ROYAL
BOTANIC
GARDENS
KEW

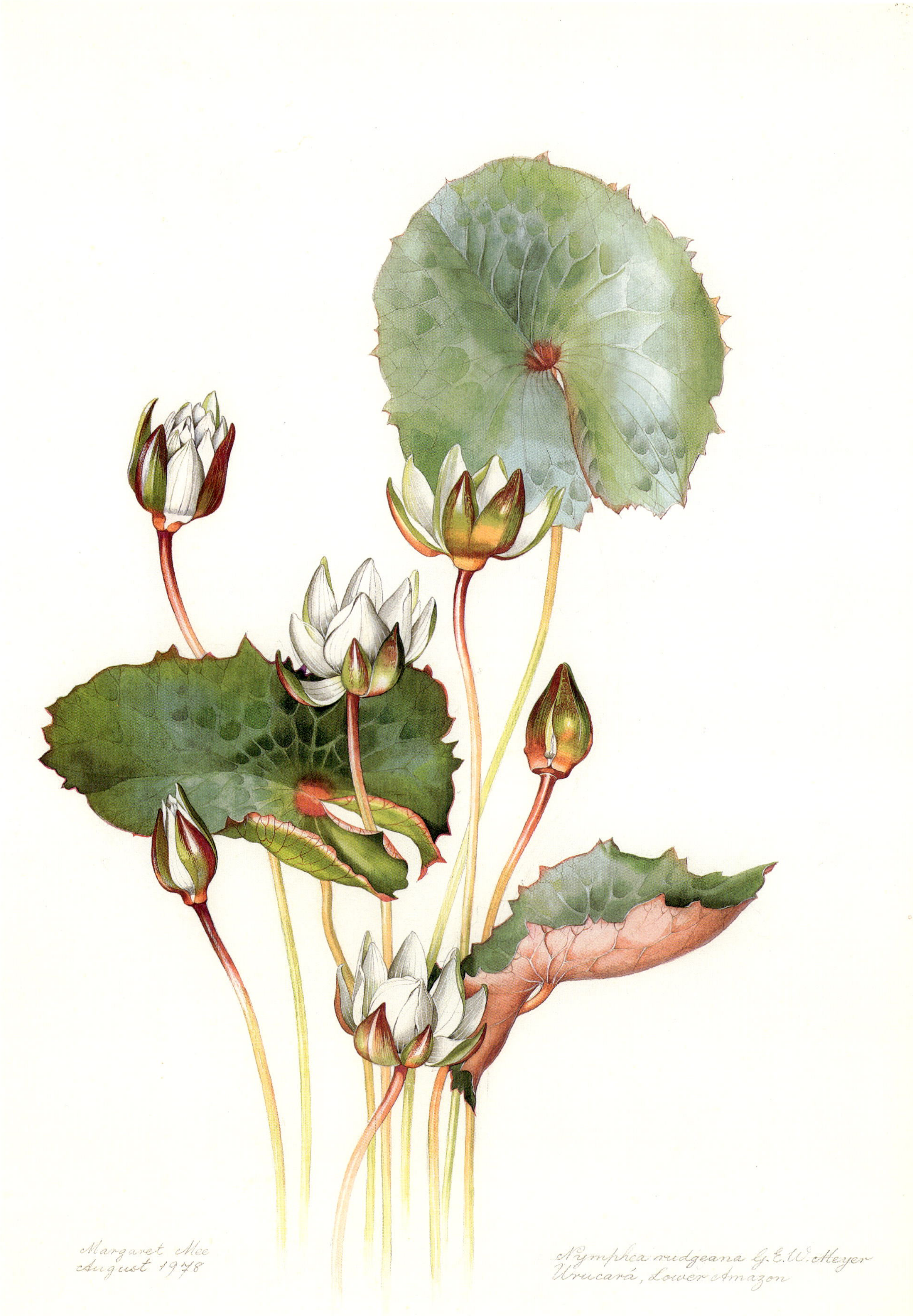
Margaret Mee
August 1978
Nymphea rudgeana G.E.W. Meyer
Urucará, Lower Amazon

The Flowering Amazon

Margaret Mee Paintings

from the Royal Botanic Gardens, Kew

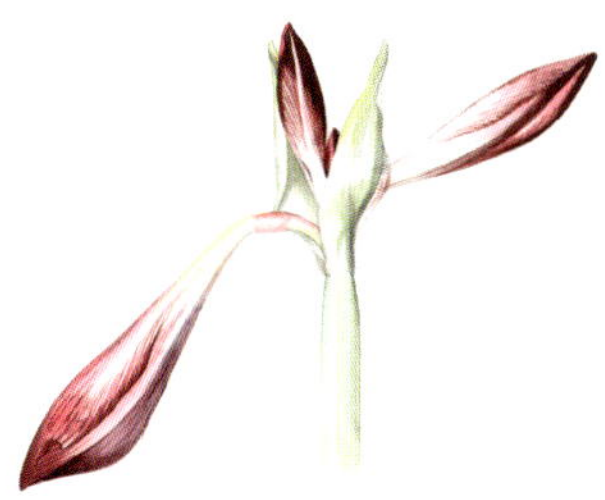

Ruth L. A. Stiff

Foreword by Professor Peter R. Crane FRS

With contributions from
Dr. Simon Mayo, Ray Desmond, Dr. Brinsley Burbidge,
and Dr. Shirley Sherwood

Royal Botanic Gardens, Kew
2004

Exhibition Venues

The William D. Rondina and Giovani Foroni LoFaro Gallery
New York Botanical Garden
Bronx, New York

The Hunt Institute for Botanical Documentation
Carnegie Mellon University
Pittsburgh, Pennsylvania

Patrick & Beatrice Haggerty Museum of Art
Marquette University
Milwaukee, Wisconsin

Gibbes Museum of Art
Charleston, South Carolina

Chicago Botanic Garden
Glencoe, Illinois

Arizona Sonora Desert Museum
Tucson, Arizona

Foreword

Margaret Mee and her paintings have become powerful symbols for plant conservation, and particularly, of the Brazilian Amazon rainforests. The story of her dramatic and adventurous life is now better known thanks to her diaries (edited by Tony Morrison, *Margaret Mee: In Search of Flowers of the Amazon Forests*, Nonsuch Expeditions, 1988) and Ruth Stiff's *Margaret Mee: Return to the Amazon* (Royal Botanic Gardens, Kew, 1996). Margaret Mee's life's work stands at the meeting point of art, science and conservation. She participated actively in all three fields, and though primarily an artist with an artist's vision, she deployed her potent abilities to wide and lasting effect. Having committed her remarkable artistic talent to the benefit of botany, she then set out to reach the hearts and minds of a wider public and in this she was extremely successful, particularly in Brazil.

The paintings reflect her very personal response to the Brazilian rainforests in which she travelled; as exquisite expressions of Nature's beauty they will surely always capture and hold the fascinated gaze of the onlooker and conjure up at once a longing, a *saudade*, for that primaeval wilderness. These are no thought experiments. Margaret Mee went to the forests and braved the messy hardships of remote exploration to bring us back these visions. And the same bold spirit that led her into the Amazon forest impelled her into the public arena as an effective advocate for its conservation.

In the last few years of her life Margaret took the steps that created her living legacy, and from that time the Royal Botanic Gardens, Kew, together with many of Margaret's friends, played a leading role. The key organizations are the Brazilian Margaret Mee Foundation (Fundação Botânica Margaret Mee) in Rio de Janeiro and the Margaret Mee Fellowship Programme, created with Margaret's active support in the last year of her life and based at the Royal Botanic Gardens, Kew. The living legacy also includes the continuing series of exhibitions, in Brazil, the United States and Britain. The goal is to take Margaret's inspiration into the future by supporting the work of younger generations dedicated to the conservation of Brazil's fabulous natural heritage. Since 1989, more than seventy Margaret Mee International Fellowships have been awarded to young Brazilian scientists and botanical artists to study in Britain, mainly at Kew. These have been funded by donations from a wide range of organizations

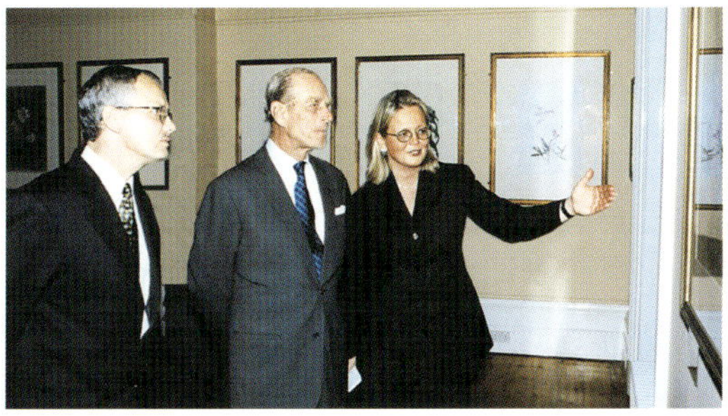

A. MCROBB, RBG KEW

HRH Prince Philip, Duke of Edinburgh, Professor Peter Crane and Ruth Stiff at a private showing of the exhibition in 2001.

In 1987, the Royal Botanic Gardens, Kew established an international travelling exhibitions programme, with paintings drawn from its extensive collections. Over the ensuing years, numerous exhibits have been mounted, showing the ephemeral beauty of the flowering world. *The Flowering Amazon: Margaret Mee Paintings from the Royal Botanic Gardens, Kew* was originally exhibited at Kew in a private showing in 2001 for HRH Prince Philip, Duke of Edinburgh. I am delighted that these remarkable paintings will now be seen by a wider audience in the United States.

Professor Peter Crane FRS
Director, Royal Botanic Gardens, Kew

Acknowledgements

In 1990, two years after Margaret Mee's untimely death, I had the unique privilege of travelling to Rio with the sole purpose of meeting with many of Mee's friends and colleagues, including the late Roberto Burle Marx, renowned landscape architect. After attending an event at the home of Burle Marx, I spent a moment at the end of the evening to reminisce with him about the many remarkable experiences he had shared with Margaret Mee. "Margaret gave me…she gave me…" After hesitating a moment longer, he raised both hands in the air and exclaimed with a mixture of awe and sadness, "she gave me fertility!"

Margaret Mee had the ability to inspire those around her to achieve more than they otherwise thought possible; to create, to discover, to explore, to care, to seek, to produce, to persevere. I would like to thank those individuals who have kept her vision alive by working so diligently on this exhibition and associated catalogue.

My colleagues at the Royal Botanic Gardens, Kew extended themselves once again to an extraordinary degree to ensure the success of the project. I am particularly indebted to the Director, Professor Peter Crane, who, from the outset, shared my vision for the exhibition. He and his wife Elinor have been unstinting in their kind support. I acknowledge with gratitude the help of John Flanagan, Head of the Library, and his most supportive staff. Marilyn Ward, Illustrations Curator, deserves special recognition. With skill, patience and efficiency, she provided expert assistance and advice throughout the planning of this exhibition. I am grateful to the Illustrations team, in particular James Kay and Samantha Cox, for their readiness to help at all times, to Julia Steele for her useful suggestions on the selection of Spruce artifacts, to Simon Mayo for his kind assistance with taxonomic questions, and to Jonathan Farley for preparing the exhibition for travel. The catalogue would never have been realized without the generous help of Alyson Prior and John Harris. Special thanks also to Jeff Eden, for his elegant catalogue design and to Andrew McRobb and Paul Little for their excellent photography.

My most affectionate thanks go to Greville and Elizabeth Mee, not only for lending to the exhibition, but also for sharing so freely their cherished memories of Margaret. I owe a debt of gratitude to Shirley Sherwood for generously lending artworks from her superb collection and for enriching the catalogue with her essay. Appreciative thanks are also due to Ray Desmond, Brinsley Burbidge, Simon Mayo, Kate Edmondson, Tony Morrison, Laura Gates, Gren and Shirley Lucas, Michael and Juliet Daly, and Joel and Laura Oppenheimer for their valuable contributions. Special thanks also to Victoria Matthews for her encouragement and sympathetic editing and to Stephen Saitas for his handsome installation design.

I am especially grateful to my sister, Ellen Therrien, my mother-in-law, Eugenia Stiff, and my dear friends, Mary Feind, Pia Pearce, and Deborah Bliss, whose insight and stability are truly gifts to treasure.

Finally, I would like to express my deepest gratitude to my husband, Enoch, and my sons, Tyler, Andrew and Christian, for their constant encouragement and unfailing support.

Contents

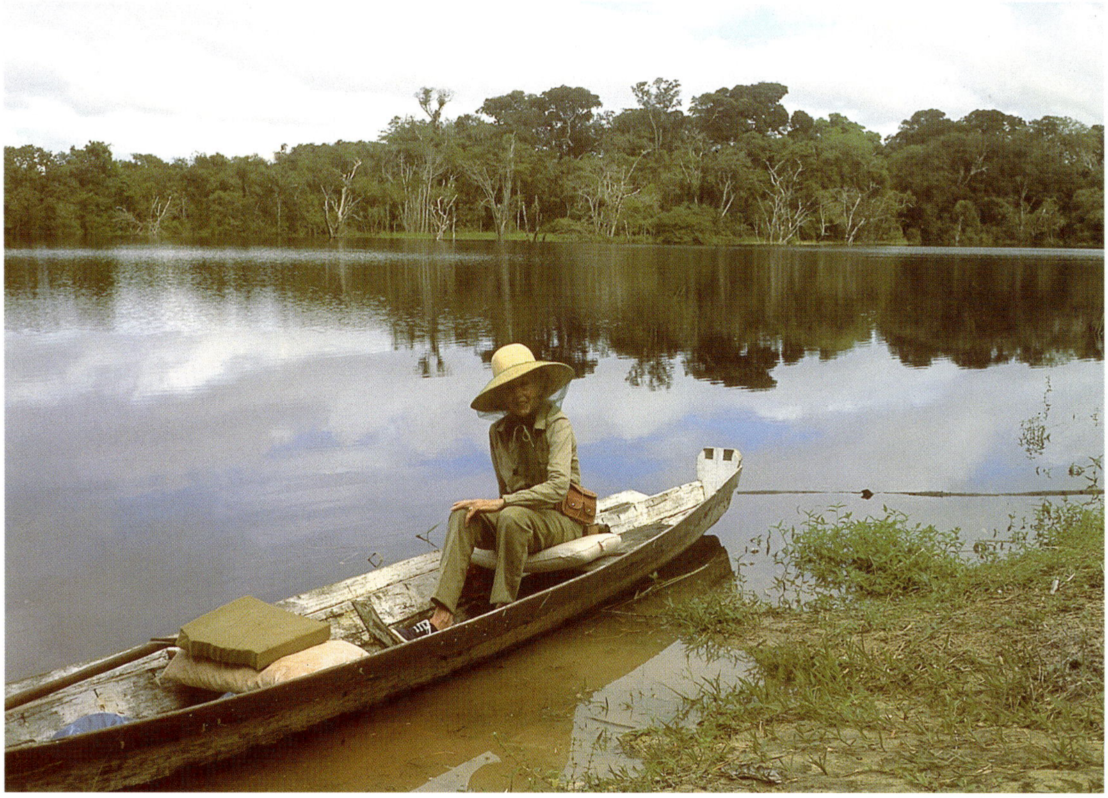

TONY MORRISON

Margaret Mee on the Rio Negro on her fifteenth expedition to Amazonia.

Introduction

The intrepid Englishwoman, Margaret Ursula Mee (1909-1988), ranks as one of the most remarkable women of the twentieth century. Referred to as the premier female explorer of the Brazilian rainforest, she was also an outstanding botanical artist, acclaimed worldwide by botanists and art critics alike. Arriving in Brazil from England in 1952, at the age of forty-three, she was initially drawn to the lush tropical flora of the southern coastal mountains, the Serra do Mar, where she began to paint the native bromeliads of the Atlantic forests.

Four years later, however, the beauty and diversity of the great Amazon basin captivated her interest. Following in the footsteps of such indomitable British explorers as Richard Spruce, Alfred Russel Wallace, and Henry Walter Bates, Margaret Mee journeyed throughout Amazonia for more than three decades.

Often paddling long distances in small, dugout canoes with a single Indian guide, Mee learned to live with the forest and its plants, animals and people. She would often live for weeks with the Tucano Indians, sharing their food and garnering information about the trees and plants she encountered on her journeys.

Mee endured great hardships, becoming dangerously ill with malaria, infectious hepatitis, and numerous unknown tropical fevers. She was abandoned and given up for dead, nearly drowned on several occasions and at one point, had her life threatened by a group of belligerent, marauding *garimpeiros* (gold prospectors).

Despite all this, an indomitable force took her always on and on to learn more about the forest flowers and immortalize them with her brush. She remained convinced that accuracy and authenticity required both the observation and painting of the plants in their natural habitat. Her working method, therefore, started with detailed sketches of the plant while in the forest. Her paints, carried in a small wooden box in her rucksack, were carefully mixed to achieve exactly the right hue, with notations on the plant's colour, locality, and habitat recorded in her diaries. This was followed by the collection of living plants whenever possible. Her husband, Greville Mee, also an artist, described her working method as follows:

> *Her favourite, indeed only method of working was to make numerous studies of every petal and leaf, the plant's form, growth and ambient without which, she said, it was not possible to make a true portrait of a flower – this attitude possibly being the result of earlier studies of art history as she was greatly impressed by the old masters' methods of working and reworking, sketching and altering until they arrived at the final painting.*

Once sketched, the plants were brought back to Rio de Janeiro, where the paintings were worked up as finished compositions in her studio. Plant groups such as orchids and bromeliads were favoured, as they could be more readily collected and flowered in cultivation. The field notes and sketches thus became an important complement to the final painting, as they allowed her to portray the flower as it was first seen in the wild.

Mee worked in gouache. Using numerous thin layers of paint, applied very deliberately and carefully, Mee's technique resembles that used for watercolour. Her paintings, celebrated for their luminosity and strength, combine meticulous observation and detailed scientific accuracy with elegant composition and confident handling of plant structure. When her paintings were seen in London for the first time in 1960, Wilfrid Blunt, the internationally recognized authority on botanical art, remarked, "they are splendid, magnificently composed, superbly reproduced … and can stand without shame in the high company of such eighteenth-century masters as Georg Dionysius Ehret, and Redouté."

Her genius allowed her to isolate an individual plant from the teeming dark mesh of giant trees, roots and vines and to portray, on a single sheet of paper, all of its forms – bud, leaf, flower, fruit. Mee had an amazing ability to capture the papery texture and distinctive curl of a leaf, describe the way blossoms cascade down a stem, and accurately delineate the fleshy bulge of a pseudobulb or the mottled stripes flanking the spine of a leaf. To scientists, Mee's paintings are better than photographs which are limited by imperfections in the sample the photographer has to shoot. Her paintings distil the essential features of the species, summarizing many patient observations in a single painting.

Mee's expeditions to Amazonia between 1956 and 1988 coincided with the period of maximum deforestation in the region, particularly during the 1970s and 1980s. A pioneering conservationist, Mee became one of the first to raise a voice against the destructive exploitation of the Amazon. With her characteristic courage and disregard for personal safety, she challenged the blind sanctioning of indiscriminate deforestation and became one of Amazonia's foremost defenders. Her indomitable spirit earned her affection and respect, particularly in Brazil but also around the world.

Driven by a passionate need to communicate a conservation message through her work, Mee began to depict the destroyed forest in her sketches and added forest backgrounds to several of her later plant portraits, seeking to impress on the observer the interdependency of forest species and the importance of preserving their natural habitats.

She remained an important international spokeswoman for conservation, widely known for her outspoken views on the destructive exploitation of Amazonia, until her death. Mee left behind more than four hundred folio gouache compositions, fifteen diaries, and forty sketchbooks packed with detailed drawings and paintings made in the field. Today, nine plants new to science bear her name.

Her legacy continues with the Margaret Mee Fellowship Programme established by Kew, and the Funcação Botânica Margaret Mee, located in Rio de Janeiro. Together they sponsor the education and training of young botanical artists and scientists from Brazil. The success of the Margaret Mee Fellowship Programme is evident in the two works by Margaret Mee scholars included in the exhibition.

The Flowering Amazon is presented in Margaret Mee's honour and is dedicated to her vision.

Ruth L. A. Stiff FLS
Curator, North American Exhibitions
Royal Botanic Gardens, Kew

Royal Botanic Gardens, Kew: A Brief History

The history of the Royal Botanic Gardens at Kew extends back over two and a half centuries, the Garden itself being symbolised by the Georgian Pagoda and the Victorian Palm House. Both were erected at a time of radical remodelling of its landscape which evolved from the union of two contiguous royal estates: Richmond Lodge, a retreat of King George II and Queen Caroline, and the White House, the country residence of their son, Frederick Prince of Wales.

Frederick planned an ambitious lay-out for his garden, and after his premature death in 1751, his widow Princess Augusta set about implementing her late husband's intentions. The statesman Lord Bute, himself a competent botanist and gardener, probably introduced her to the young architect William Chambers. From 1757 to 1763, Chambers imaginatively fulfilled Frederick's vision of an exotic Kew with classical and oriental buildings of which the Pagoda is the best-known survivor. Artists painted Kew, foreigners included it in their tour of England, and other European gardens imitated it. A modest botanic garden of just nine acres, laid out in 1759, hinted at its future role.

When Augusta died in 1772, her eldest son, King George III, inherited the property and eventually merged it with the grounds of Richmond Lodge. The royal family were regular visitors, and the King indulged his agricultural interests which he shared with Joseph Banks, a Lincolnshire landowner.

Banks had accompanied Captain Cook on his round-the-world voyage on HMS *Endeavour*, and was introduced to the King after his return. He once boasted to the Spanish ambassador that he held "a kind of superintendence" at Kew where on most Saturdays he inspected the estate with His Majesty, no doubt making discreet suggestions and listening attentively to any royal comments. He aimed to grow an unrivalled display of flowers, ensuring that "as many of the new plants as possible should make their first appearance in the Royal Gardens".

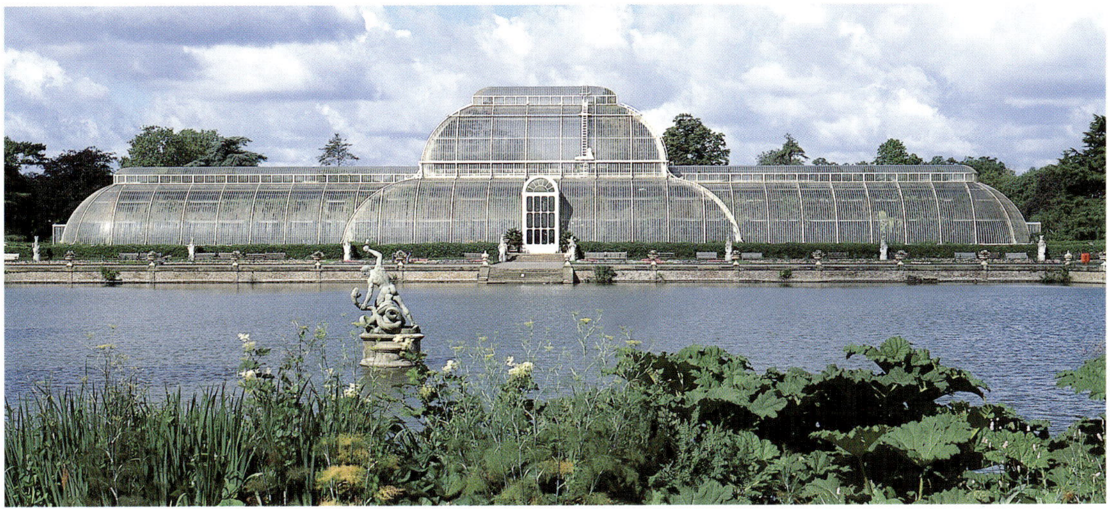

A. MCROBB, RBG KEW

The Palm House, designed by Decimus Burton, was completed in 1848.

One of the gardeners, Francis Masson, was sent to the Cape of Good Hope in South Africa in 1772, the first of Kew's plant collectors. He brought back *Ericas, Ixias, Pelargoniums, Stapelias* and much else. His cycad, *Encephalartos altensteinii*, shipped in 1775, is still being cosseted in a tub in the Palm House. Banks recruited other collectors from the royal gardeners: Peter Good went to Australia and William Kerr to Canton; James Bowie and Allan Cunningham collected together in Brazil, then separated, Bowie going to the Cape and Cunningham to Australia. Banks persuaded diplomats, army and naval personnel, merchants and missionaries to collect seeds for Kew whilst travelling abroad. Soon its glasshouses overflowed with floral exotics evoking the admiration and envy of continental botanists and gardeners.

With Banks's death in 1820, Kew lost the dynamism and sense of purpose that had made it a botanic garden of international distinction. Coming perilously close to being closed, it was saved only by the forceful recommendations of a specially convened working party in 1838. Its chairman, John Lindley, urged that it should be reconstituted as a National Botanic Garden responsible for advising on official gardens in the colonies. The government somewhat reluctantly accepting this proposal, in 1841 appointed Sir William Jackson Hooker, Professor of Botany at Glasgow University, a director of the small botanic garden originally created for Princess Augusta. The head gardener, W.T. Aiton, retained control of the rest of the former royal estate.

Hooker's priority had to be the acquisition of more space. He gradually encroached on Aiton's domain, taking all of it in 1845 when Aiton finally retired. Existing glasshouses were restored or replaced and the building of a new Palm House sanctioned. This magnificent curvilinear glasshouse, designed by the architect Decimus Burton and the structural engineer Richard Turner, exuberantly proclaims Victorian skill and competence.

Government officials generally perceived Kew as little more than a large public park. Hooker needed all his guile and diplomacy to launch the scientific initiatives he envisaged. He generously made his own herbarium, one of the largest in private possession, available to visiting botanists. He created the first British museum of economic botany, with his own specimens as its foundation. He revived Banks's policy of sending plant collectors abroad (including his son Joseph, who went to the Himalayas to find new rhododendrons and alpines). Always lacking adequate funds, he persuaded shipping companies to transport live plants free of freightage charges.

The Colonial Office consulted him about the establishment and management of botanic gardens in the British Empire. Kew propagated and shipped small consignments of useful plants to the colonies. The India Office enlisted his help when Cinchona plants were being transferred from South America to India, where they were to be grown as a source of quinine for British troops stationed there.

Sir William Hooker transformed Kew Gardens into a major centre for the study of the world's flora, an institution where new species were identified and classified and where the gardens and glasshouses displayed many new discoveries. Kew became one of London's most popular public gardens, attracting thousands of visitors.

Its participation in imperial affairs intensified when Joseph Hooker succeeded his father as Director in 1865. He grandly described it as "the botanical headquarters of the British Empire and its dependencies". It supplied plants and seeds to the colonies and supervised the transfer of economic crops between them, including arranging the arrival of vast consignments of rubber seeds from Brazil and the dispatch of seedlings to India and later to Malaya.

During W. T. Thiselton-Dyer's term as Director (1885-1905), Kew provided economic intelligence on the growing of crops in the Empire. The Colonial Office, the Foreign Office and the India Office automatically turned to him for advice and practical help. In 1902, he became botanical adviser to the Secretary of State for the Colonies.

With the independence of the former British colonies, Kew gradually found another international role in surveying and listing the flora of poorer nations, and in formulating schemes to protect threatened species. A modest seed bank established at Kew in 1967 solely for exchange with other botanic gardens has developed into the Millennium Seed Bank officially opened by

HRH The Prince of Wales in 2002. Seeds harvested from some of the world's most endangered habitats by Kew staff or local collectors are stored in underground vaults at a temperature of -20°C. By 2010, Kew hopes to have banked seeds representing about ten per cent of the world's flora. It has been described as a Noah's Ark, where seeds will remain viable for many years and be available for planting in any future regeneration programmes. "The better management of the earth's environment by increasing knowledge and understanding of the plant and fungal kingdoms" has become Kew's credo.

Kew's scientific achievements and its conservation work undoubtedly influenced UNESCO's decision in 2003 to award Kew the prestigious World Heritage Site status. However, it was primarily given in recognition of Kew's reputation as an historic landscape, boasting a royal palace, fine Georgian garden architecture, and two magnificent Victorian conservatories.

Kew proudly accepts its responsibility for this cultural inheritance while pursuing other objectives in the preservation and display of living plants, in conservation, research and in education. Since the late eighteenth century, it has also been a centre for botanical art. For over 160 years Kew botanists have edited *Curtis's Botanical Magazine*, the world's oldest floral journal with coloured reproductions of paintings by contemporary artists. It is thus appropriate that Margaret Mee's superb plant portraits, sketches and notebooks should be incorporated in the Kew Library's collection of some 200,000 original paintings, drawings and engravings of flowers. They join the journals, field notes and plant lists of Richard Spruce (1817-93) who explored and botanised in the Andes and Amazon basin. Mee followed Spruce in the upper Rio Negro and even sketched some of the plants he discovered there.

When Marianne North (1830-90) was seeking a suitable repository for more than 800 of her oil paintings of the world's flora, she offered them to Kew and, furthermore, provided an art gallery in which to display them. She was a compulsive traveller, who included Brazil in her itinerary. Both she and Mee painted plants in their natural habitats, stoically enduring the discomforts of climate and insects. Both cared passionately about the environment, especially Mee who deplored the destruction of the Amazon rainforests. The Audubon Society included her in their top 100 twentieth-century conservationists.

Since the time of Kew's first interest in Brazil's flora, there have been frequent scientific expeditions there. Today Kew is collaborating with Brazilian botanists to help the people of the semi-arid north-east of the country to make better use of their vegetation. Kew now administers the Margaret Mee Fellowship Programme, which trains Brazilian botanical artists and encourages research on Amazonian plants and their conservation.

Ray Desmond
Author and former Chief Librarian and Archivist,
Royal Botanic Gardens, Kew

Margaret Mee: A Biographical Tribute

In 1976 I found myself, a greenhorn botanist, in the tropics for the first time. We had landed at Rio *en route* to Bahia and our expedition leader Ray Harley, an old friend of Margaret and Greville Mee, called them from the airport in the hope of an early morning cup of tea. Soon we were winding our way up into Santa Teresa, the old suburb that cascades down steep slopes towards the city centre, and eventually we arrived in Rua Julio Otoni at the Mee's distinctive house, perched on a precipitous slope in the midst of large jackfruit trees. The sensations of those first few hours in Brazil are forever associated with Margaret and Greville's garden and street: the deafening siren of morning cicadas, brilliant sun on white walls, the weight of the heat and humidity, and a rich profusion of vegetation out of which sprang scarlet and purple bromeliad spikes. Plants seemed to sprout from every possible point, regardless of form and decorum, a veritable mirror to the spirit of the city: dramatic, exotic, graceful and seductive – perfect poised beauty suddenly encountered, anciently wise and anciently dangerous.

In the midst of this riot, Margaret's gentle stooping figure greeted us, fussing over Greville and the dangers of the street. As we talked, the names of the famous and adventurous were thick in the air – Richard Evans Schultes, Ghillean Prance, João Murça Pires, William Rodrigues, Walter Egler, Adolfo Ducke, Richard Spruce, Robin Hanbury-Tenison, and many others. Margaret had very clear large blue eyes that were totally beguiling. She seemed fragile; I thought her rather elderly and frail – but suddenly she would erupt into a giggle about some story or event, and her youthful spirit shone forth.

Within an hour or two, eminent persons began to gather. In the space of a single day I met Dr. Aristides Leão – the President of Brazil's Academy of Sciences, Dr. Guido Pabst the orchid specialist, Dr. Graziela Barroso – Brazil's most eminent botanist, and Roberto Burle Marx – the world-famous landscape artist. This all took place as though previously planned, but it had in fact been improvised with the casual, easy etiquette that is characteristic of Rio. The talk was of the Amazon, the forest, the destruction, the discovery of new plants and their secrets. Margaret had an inexhaustible enthusiasm for plants and the forest and a gift for conveying the pure excitement of the discovery of a new flower. Her discovery was your discovery. She was entirely free of that tendency so common in naturalists to hunt, to trap, to keep and hoard. Margaret discovered rather than hunted, and communicated her discovery like a vision made with new eyes. Her power was to reveal. Her great friend and mentor, Roberto Burle Marx, expressed this perfectly: "...to seek out a plant, bring it from its obscurity and reveal it to those who are inspired by Nature, is a true discovery..."

The atmosphere in Margaret's house seemed almost old-world. Classical music floated up from the sitting room below, where Greville played his huge collection of LPs. It seemed a paradise of elegant repose, until, opening the front gate, the visitor was whisked into the turbulent, electric current of Rio's street life, with its sensation of heart-stopping excitement or danger at every corner.

First impressions were deceptive: her home, so peaceful and cultured in contrast to the rigours of the frontier life on which she thrived; her fear of Rio's streets, when her indomitable courage shone so bright and strong; her bird-like physique, which endured and overcame hardships that have defeated so many; her paintings of beautiful plants, seemingly eternal denizens of limitless forests – but in reality visions of a vanishing era, of plants and forests disappearing into oblivion. Margaret had enormous charisma, a special poise and energy, and a quick and whole-hearted compassion. She was loved by many who knew her, particularly in Brazil.

In the introduction to her diaries (*Margaret Mee: In Search of Flowers of the Amazon Forests*,

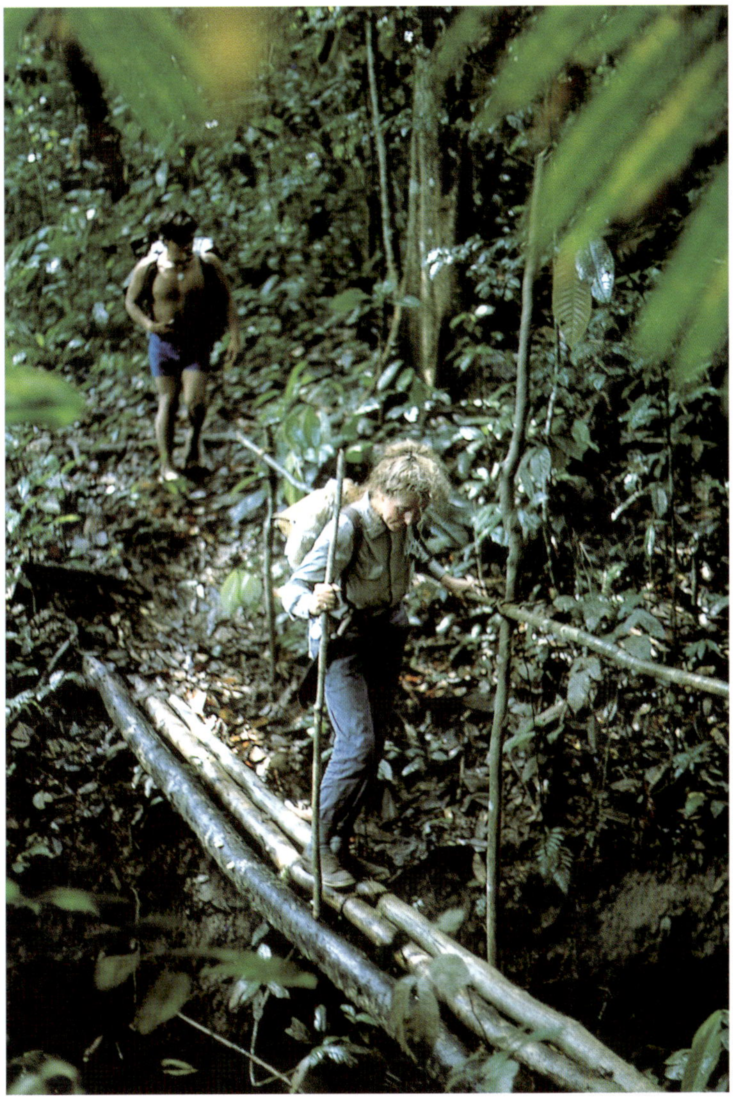

OTIS IMBODEN, NATIONAL GEOGRAPHIC IMAGE COLLECTION

Margaret Mee during her 1967 expedition to the Pico da Neblina, the highest peak on the upper Rio Negro.

Nonesuch Expeditions, 1988.) Tony Morrison has given us the best published account of Margaret's life, from her birth in 1909 near Chesham in southern England, to shortly before her death. Here it is clear that her character was forged in other, earlier tests. Many of the qualities that underpin her Amazon endeavours had already been evident in her twenties when she threw herself into the politics and dangers of left wing opposition to fascism in the inter-war period. As a young trade unionist she made an impressive showing as a public speaker, committed to strong ideals with the fortitude to endure hardships along the way. Her risky travels to Berlin and France in the thirties also testify to a devil-may-care adventurousness. Margaret was no solemn, humourless zealot, but a free spirit. Morrison's account suggests that the stories of her globe-trotting grandfather John Henry Churchman may have been an influence.

She showed her artistic talent early, fostered by her Aunt Nell, a children's book illustrator; later she went to Art School in Watford, north of London. It seems inescapable, as Tony Morrison's biography suggests, that her childhood and adolescence in the English countryside should have left their mark in her love for nature. But politics and the war intervened, pushing aside other considerations and it wasn't until peace came in 1945 that she picked up the trail of her vocation, attending St. Martin's School of Art and, in 1947, Camberwell School of Art, where she became a prize-winning pupil of Victor Pasmore. At this time she began to acquire the marvellous technical expertise later put to work in the Brazilian Amazon, though real plant painting was still to come.

In 1952, Margaret and Greville went to São Paulo, then still relatively small and provincial. Margaret taught art, and Greville built up a commercial art business. It was here that Margaret discovered her métier as a plant portraitist. She was overwhelmed by the beauty of the Atlantic coastal forests of the Rio and São Paulo regions, which even as late as the 1950s, were still very extensive. Rich in epiphytes and ferns, many of the world's best-known ornamental plants were first collected there. Margaret, Grevillle, and their Dutch friend Rita de Pagter often hiked into the forested hills and vales of the Serra do Mar. Margaret began to focus on plant portraits, and was soon drawn to the challenge of the Amazon, the mightiest tropical forest of them all.

She embarked on her true career with her first journey to Amazonia, a shoestring affair with Rita, in 1956 when Margaret was already forty-six. Thus, in middle age she began a risky and adventurous new life with all the eager enthusiasm of an eighteen-year-old. The experience was crucial. On Margaret's return to São Paulo, her work advanced apace and ensuing exhibitions in São Paulo and Rio de Janeiro (1958) and in London (1960) established her as a remarkable new botanical artist. The Rio exhibition brought about a crucial introduction to Roberto Burle Marx, who became a close friend.

The flora of Brazil is almost certainly the richest of any one nation on the planet. In 1840, the German botanist Karl von Martius initiated *Flora Brasiliensis*, an immense book finally completed in 1906, with some 23,000 species. In 1940, Dr. Frederico Carlos Hoehne, founder of the São Paulo Botanical Institute, began a revised version and Margaret was invited to illustrate the bromeliad volume. She began this work in 1960 and travelled throughout Brazil alongside the bromeliad expert Dr. Lyman Smith, rapidly acquiring specialist knowledge of bromeliads and a particular ability to paint them. She later discovered various new Amazonian species, several of which were named after her. Her fifty-nine bromeliad paintings were published by the São Paulo Institute of Botany in 1992.

Roberto Burle Marx became an increasingly important influence through their common concern for the forest conservation. At his urging, she and Greville moved to Rio. She became passionately concerned for the preservation of the Amerindian peoples, the Amazon forest and its wildlife. This led to outspoken public statements; with Burle Marx, she brought these issues to public attention and it is a measure of the affection and esteem in which she was held in Brazil that this had no ill effects. President Geisel opened her 1977 Brasília exhibition and later she was awarded Brazil's Order of the Southern Cross.

Margaret made fifteen journeys to the Amazon, developing a particular affection for the Rio Negro where she made her final trip, in 1988, with Tony Morrison, to paint the night-flowering "Moonflower" cactus (*Selenicereus wittii*). By the 1980s, Margaret had formed an Amazon Collection, destined for a major public institution. The sale of these sixty paintings was resolved by the happy intervention of the Hon. Christopher McLaren. During a trip to Brazil, he was so impressed by Margaret's work that he returned to the UK convinced of the need to secure the collection for posterity. Through his persistence, the Royal Botanic Gardens, Kew began to consider the question seriously.

Thus it was that in January 1988, I found myself once again at the Mee's, this time with Tony Morrison, who was working with Margaret on her diaries. Tony suggested forming a Trust, to campaign for funds. The Amazon was in the news and the time seemed ripe. Margaret enthusiastically took up Kew's suggestion of a travelling fellowship scheme for young Brazilian botanical artists and botanists. Thus the germ of the Margaret Mee Amazon Trust was born. Sir William Harding, former British Ambassador to Brazil, agreed to lead the Trust, and with Grenville Lucas, then Keeper of the Herbarium at Kew, and Christopher McLaren, the Trust was soon in existence and the campaign began.

Many of Margaret's friends came forward to help. Ghillean Prance, then Kew's Director, gave a tremendous boost to the campaign. In November 1988 Margaret's diaries were published, and the Trust was officially launched at the preview of her Amazon Exhibition at Kew. Margaret gave an electrifying lecture at the Royal Geographical Society to a packed house, then made a whistle-stop tour to the United States, appearing on the MacNeil-Lehrer News Hour. Despite her seventy-nine years, Margaret took everything in her stride, she seemed radiantly energetic and her message was getting through everywhere. At this exciting moment, disaster struck. Margaret was killed in a car accident in Leicestershire on 30 November 1988.

When the news reached Brazil, the reaction was immediate. At a moving commemorative tribute, her many friends and colleagues initiated Brazil's Fundação Botânica Margaret Mee. Under the leadership of Philip Jenkins, the Fundação prospered, buoyed up by tremendous support from people all over Brazil. The Fundação fights for Amazon conservation, continues Margaret's adventurous approach to botanical illustration, encourages and stimulates young Brazilians to take up the challenge of the Amazon, and educates the public through Margaret's superb paintings.

The work of the Trust (now the Margaret Mee Fellowship Programme) and the Fundação has since been tremendously successful. The funds to purchase Margaret's paintings, diaries and sketchbooks were raised, and they are now in the care of Kew. Hundreds of grants have been awarded to support the work of young Brazilian illustrators and biologists in Amazonia and Atlantic Forest. Margaret's work has been shown throughout Brazil, the UK and North America, and the Fundação has expanded into conservation management in the Atlantic Forest region. Every year at Brazil's National Botanical Congress, the Margaret Mee Prize is offered by the Fundação to the most promising young botanical artist of the year. Over a hundred students have been awarded international fellowships to Kew.

Today the issues remain as urgent as during Margaret's lifetime. Amazonia is by far the largest tract of tropical forest on the planet. Its future is uncertain, and the pressures are many. It is a natural system of the utmost importance to our physical and biological future. But the human dilemma becomes ever more acute, as economic, political, and national issues have also to be addressed. Amazonia is the stage on which an enormous drama will be acted out over the coming decades. Margaret Mee played a significant part in this drama. Whatever may be the destiny of the Amazon, future generations will inherit from her a true vision of the magic and beauty of their wildwood past.

Dr. Simon Mayo
Senior Botanist, Royal Botanic Gardens, Kew

Margaret Mee: Portrait of an Artist

Though I had known the work of Margaret Mee through reproductions for many years, I did not meet her until 1987. That meeting at Kew began an all too brief association with a truly remarkable woman. The frail, rather nervous, diffident, almost bird-like person of first acquaintance didn't match the tales of expeditions and adventure in Amazonian rainforest. The knowledge that her painting kit contained a .32 revolver didn't fit. Her fragility seemed at odds with the stories of malaria and hepatitis, of encounters with belligerent Indians, of near drowning, and of accidents that left her with broken ribs. And her reputation as a forceful and tireless campaigner against the indifference which permitted the destruction of the rainforest seemed at variance with the shy, attractive and hesitant seventy-eight year old I first met.

First impressions are often deceptive, and sheer physical strength is not always a prerequisite for Amazon explorers. Margaret's inner strength and determination to paint what she loved – the plants of the rainforest – together with her passionate concern for the Amazon and its peoples compensated for and overcame her fragile nature. She was an intrepid explorer, as tough as they come, driven by a passion that made her unstoppable until a car on an English motorway did what the so-called hostile tropics could not do.

Her paintings, completed in her studio using detailed field drawings and gouache sketches drawn directly from nature, are some of the finest records of plants and their environments ever made, and are a significant milestone in the history of the botanical illustration tradition of which she was such an important part.

Botany and illustration have always gone hand in hand. Some of the earliest recognizable drawings of plants were executed to permit those seeking cures for diseases to identify the species that would help. From the fifteenth century onward, botanical artists were employed to illustrate herbals – books which catalogued the medicinal value of plants – and illustration as a record or to facilitate identification has been at the heart of botanical illustration ever since.

The rapid rise of scientific botany in the seventeenth and eighteenth centuries, coupled with increasingly sophisticated methods of book production and printing, liberated botanical painting. The rise of a wealthy merchant class, allied with an increasing enthusiasm for gardening, led to a growing demand for books of plant pictures. As a result of this demand, botanical painting was established as a profession: illustrators were needed and the seventeenth, eighteenth and nineteenth centuries produced a wealth of wonderful paintings in many media aimed at the specific audience of botany and horticulture.

The stipulation was simple and uncompromising: a fully accurate, representational picture of a plant to permit its precise identification. Every petal, leaf and stamen must be exactly as it was on the plant, colours must be faithful to nature: cold, clinical precision was everything. In most cases, the plant was illustrated against a pure white background with not a hint of the plant's connection with nature. Even the roots were washed free of soil. The only liberty permitted, the only artistic license allowed was, curiously, for the artist to "repair" an insect-chewed leaf and make the plant even more perfect, even more super-real than it was in life. The products are the true, pure botanical illustrations. Truth and purity, of course, do not always exclude beauty. In many ways truth and purity are beauty. Many of the scientific illustrations produced for this demanding audience have immense charm and often have great pictorial qualities. Many are beautiful because of the strict demands made on the illustrator.

The bulk of Margaret's phenomenal output falls in the scientific illustration category and obeys the strict demands of the tradition. Everything is shown as it is in nature – all that is missing is the background. Scientists and gardeners love her paintings as they would a

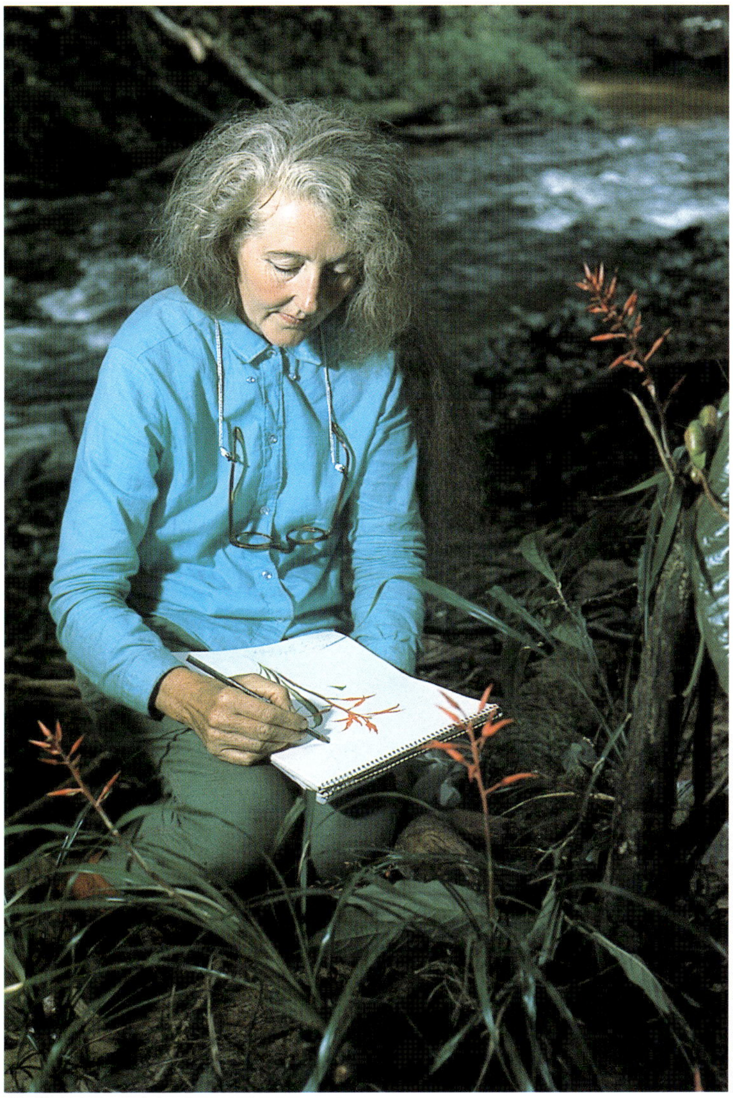

OTIS IMBODEN, NATIONAL GEOGRAPHIC IMAGE COLLECTION

Margaret Mee sketching a bromeliad during her 1967 expedition to the Pico da Neblina.

picture of an old friend. In many ways the picture is equivalent to the plant and can substitute for it. It is very rare for a botanist to fail to identify the species of plant in one of her paintings because some feature is not visible. Margaret spent much of her life with professional botanists, and she knew what they wanted. Perhaps the best known and best loved of her pictures are those of orchids, a plant family to which she gave particular attention and which she painted with consummate mastery.

If Margaret had only painted accurate representations of plants, her work would have been significant. But she did a great deal more. Her innate ability as an artist, sharpened by her time at art college learning from various artists including Victor Pasmore (co-founder along with Claude Rogers and William Coldstream of the Euston Road Group), helped her to produce superbly satisfying compositions. In fact, it is often the composition that you notice, after admiring the beauty of the plant. Surprisingly, even though she had always drawn and painted, it was not until she was almost forty that she took the formal lessons which turned her latent talent into a mature fluidity in which everything she did, even the humblest study, had style and elegance.

Running in parallel with the development of scientific botanical illustration mentioned above, was the tradition of flower painting. Flower paintings were more concerned with beauty than accuracy, and were mainly bought (and often commissioned) by collectors to hang on their walls. The tradition began with the sixteenth-century Dutch flower pieces and reached an extraordinary expressiveness with the French Impressionists. Contemporary artists continue to see flowers as great subjects for paintings. Does this very different style of painting connect at all with Margaret Mee – a veteran of fifteen Amazon expeditions and an associate of botanists?

The answer to this question lies in some of her extraordinary paintings – the ones that show plants against a pictorial backdrop. They fit right into the flower painting tradition and can hold their own with the best of the Dutch or French painters with one significant difference: in all of Margaret's paintings, you can identify the plants in the foreground and background. Her scientific imperative has won through, but has left us with paintings that can hang with full confidence in the company of those by Van Huysum, Ruysch, Van Os, Monet, Renoir and Georgia O'Keefe. It is very obvious that I rank her among the greatest botanical illustrators of all time: with these few names, I also put her firmly in the world of great artists.

Though I adore her paintings, I am captivated and enchanted by her studies and sketchbooks. It is here that we see Margaret at work, and we are very fortunate that these are an important part of this exhibition. For some reason, Margaret's studies have a completeness and an integrity which set them apart from many other studies. Even though many have only one petal or one leaf in full colour, even though some parts are only hinted at or are shown in outline, she still seems to have worked on them until they felt right. Her instinct for composition compels her to go on until the composition, however slender, works. Each study is a perfect work of art in its own right.

Very little exists in the way of published material that gives a critical review of Margaret's work. Little has also been published on the way Margaret worked except for the fact that she worked in gouache as a medium, rather than the more traditional watercolour. I find this neglect of technique significant. Technique is important to other painters who want to learn from her work and emulate what she has done, but to most of us, it is incidental. Margaret was a painter who knew how to use her talents and her tools to create something that worked. She was always willing to discuss technique with other painters, but somehow treated it with the same enthusiasm that she would give to a discussion on paddling a canoe: it was a means to an end.

Enjoy her wonderful orchids, marvel at her stunning bromeliads and fall in love with the pictures and the flowers they represent. Beyond this, be concerned that they and the world they inhabit are threatened with extinction and think what you can do to help. She would have wanted that.

Dr. Brinsley Burbidge FLS
Director, St. Croix Botanical Garden, U.S. Virgin Islands

Margaret Mee: Legacy to Botanical Painting

It is now more than fifteen years since Margaret Mee's death and yet her influence is still growing among botanical artists and environmentalists. She was one of the first people to alert the world about the dangers threatening the Amazonian rainforests – and she did this through her paintings. They were the result of her many trips into the wild, usually with only local Indian guides. On these expeditions she made preliminary sketches and collected plants, discovering several new species. She attempted to get them back to Rio so they could be cultivated by the Botanical Gardens or by Roberto Burle Marx, the world-renowned landscape gardener.

In Margaret's plant portraits, she generally placed the design beautifully on the page in a classic way, sometimes with a discreet plant dissection at the base. Her sketch books are a delight, with subtle details captured swiftly on the page. Occasionally she painted full-sized flowers against a rainforest backdrop. She produced less than a dozen such scenes and confessed to her husband, Greville, that she really preferred the more classic studies. But it is the paintings with their tropical settings that fired the public's imagination. She encouraged Brazilians to look at their own spectacular plants at a time when their fashionable gardeners were still aspiring to cultivate European plants and battling to grow roses in an alien climate.

Margaret Mee's influence on botanical artists today has been profound. She was one of the leaders of the environmental lobby and her daring solo trips have inspired many others to paint in the wild, directly from nature. In particular, the six members of the Demonte family have conducted many expeditions into the wild, camping and working in remote places all over Brazil. Etienne Demonte also has a well-established atelier in Petropolis, in the Atlantic rainforest above Rio where he has taught wildlife painting to many students.

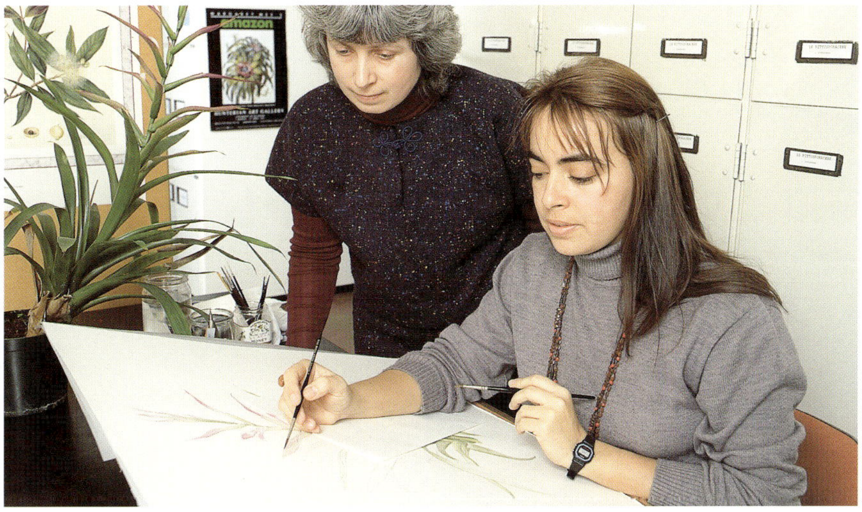

A. MCROBB, RBG KEW

Christabel King, botanical artist and teacher, with Dulce Nascimento, Margaret Mee scholar.

Alvaro Nunes is another artist who spends long periods in the wild, particularly concentrating on painting tropical fruits of the Brazilian cerrado (savannah). Trained originally as an architect, his work has both a precise and lustrous quality.

Margaret Mee's strong and dramatic plant portraits, particularly of spectacular bromeliads, have clearly influenced Malena Baretto's work with the same plants. She has produced many paintings of bromeliads and sometimes uses the contrivance of fading the large leaves near the edges of the painting to suggest their massive spread – a device often appearing in Margaret Mee's works.

There are several additional artists resident in Brazil whose interest in the field was sparked by Margaret Mee's example. Patricia Villela paints beautifully in a similar style and I particularly enjoy her strong yet subtle characterisation of tropical plants. Trained as an artist in the 1970s, she attended various botanical painting classes in the last ten years taught by Malena Barreto, Christabel King, Etienne Demonte and Katie Lee. She has become a most proficient and assured artist, painting heliconias, bromeliads and strelitzias with great skill.

After Margaret died in 1988, her many friends in Brazil and in Kew joined together to form the Margaret Mee Foundation, which facilitates the exchange of dozens of scholars between Kew and Brazil. Carefully chosen artists are sent to Kew to work with Christabel King for several months and then return home with their freshly honed skills. Some of the most recent have been Carolina de Bassi, who also trained with Etienne Demonte, Sergio Allevato, Anelise Scherer de Souza Nunes, Fatima Zagonel and Dulce Nascimento. It is always a pleasure to visit Kew at the end of their stay to admire their work and hopefully to add some to my collection. There are now four different Brazilian centres taught by Margaret Mee scholars in various parts of Brazil. I see more and more excellent work by these artists each time I visit Rio and the exhibitions arranged there by the Margaret Mee Foundation have had a steadily increasing standard of excellence.

In the Shirley Sherwood Collection, I now have work by sixteen artists who were either born in Brazil or who live and paint there. They have all been captivated by the magnificent native flora and undoubtedly influenced in various ways by Margaret Mee's life and work as an artist and a champion of the Amazon rainforest.

Margaret Mee has become an icon in South America and her life was chosen as the theme for a samba school for the Rio carnival, with three thousand eco-friendly dancers parading to a Margaret Mee theme song. There is no greater accolade than that in Brazil.

Dr. Shirley Sherwood FLS, VMM
Author and Collector
Shirley Sherwood Collection of Contemporary Botanical Art

The Catalogue

Heliconia adeliana

(family Heliconiaceae)

Pencil and gouache on paper, 1981 (66 x 48.3 cm.)
Collection: Royal Botanic Gardens, Kew

Native to Central and South America and a number of South Pacific islands, heliconias are robust, fast-growing, forest-floor herbs. Like the bananas to which they are related, heliconias may reach vast sizes, but their elegant flowering shoots give them a characteristic beauty all their own. The flowers are small and borne within large, often vividly coloured bracts (modified leaves), providing a strong visual signal for pollinating birds.

We came out of the caatinga *(a forest of short spindly trees) into a dark jungle of giant trees where scarlet heliconias grew shoulder high...*

M. Mee in T. Morrison (ed.), *Margaret Mee: In Search of Flowers of the Amazon Forests*

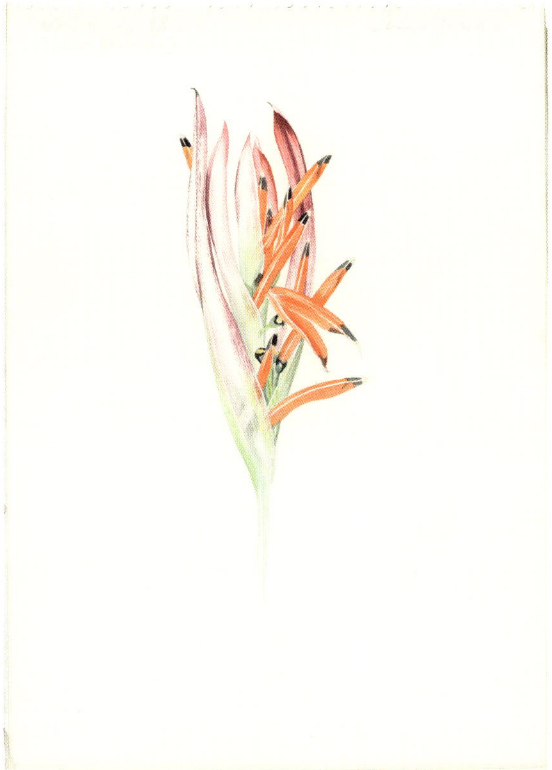

Heliconia adeliana, field sketch

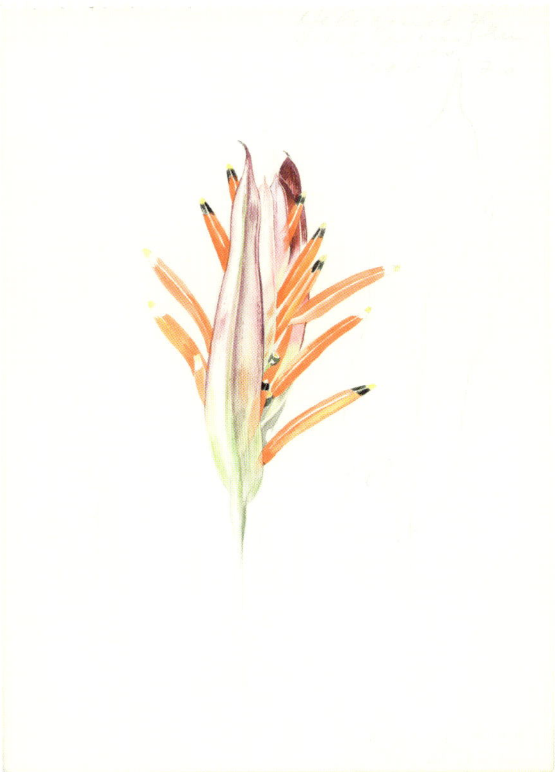

Heliconia adeliana, field sketch

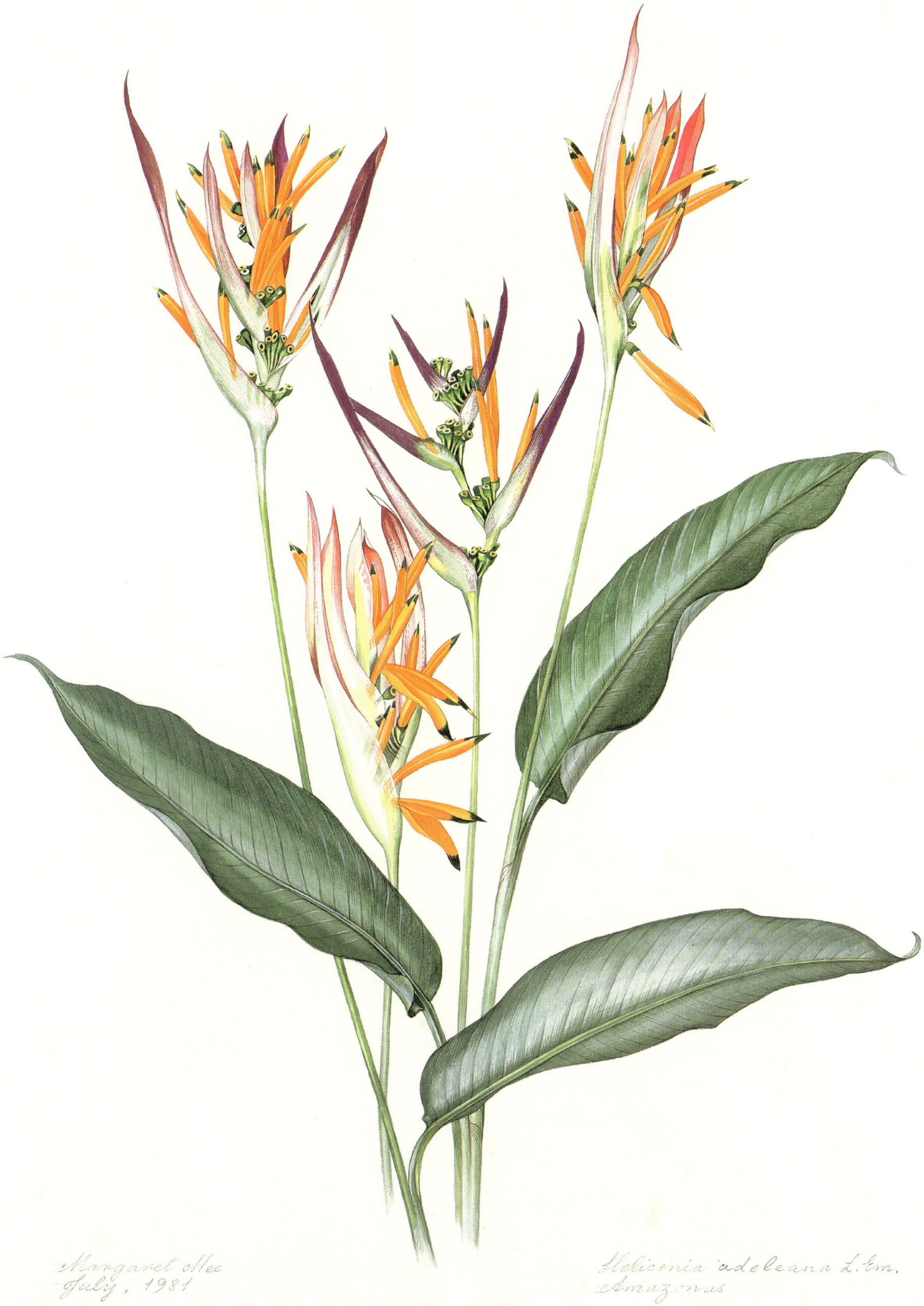
Margaret Mee
July, 1981
Heliconia adeleana L. Em.
Amazonas

Gustavia augusta

(family Lecythidaceae)

Pencil and gouache on paper, 1985 (72.4 x 50.5 cm.)
Collection: Royal Botanic Gardens, Kew

Reaching a height of approximately 65 feet, *Gustavia augusta* can be found along river margins and other habitats with periodically flooded soil. The genus *Gustavia* was founded on this species in 1775 by the Swedish botanist Carl Linnaeus, who established the universal scientific system of plant nomenclature. He dedicated the new genus to Gustav III, the Swedish king who supported Linnaeus in his botanical quests.

In this complex and striking composition, Mee depicts *Gustavia augusta* within its natural habitat of epiphytic aroids, orchids, and bromeliads. The hanging nests of the oropendula bird, the arches of the *Mauritia* palm, and the white egret lend elegance to the scene.

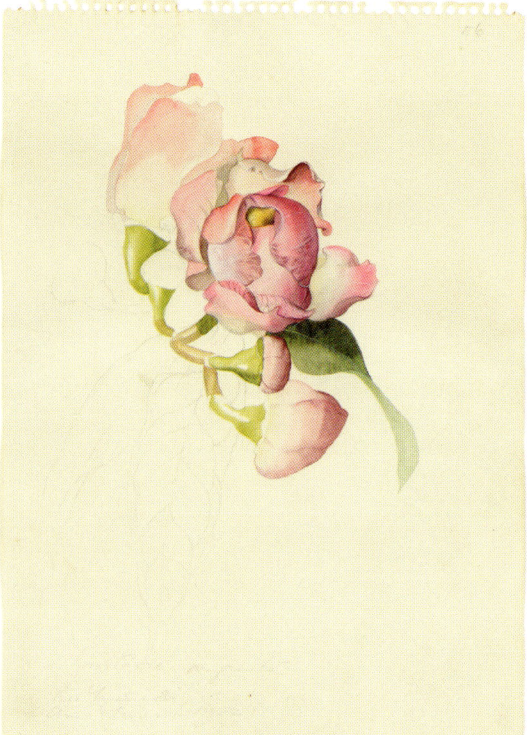

Gustavia augusta, field sketch

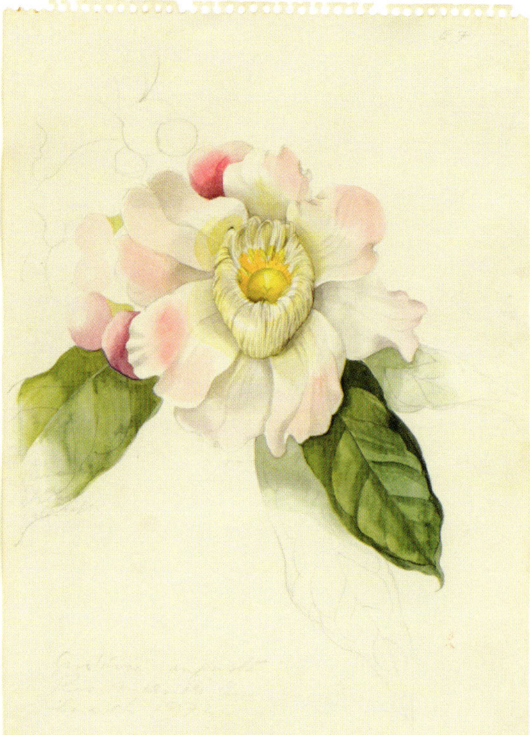

Gustavia augusta, field sketch

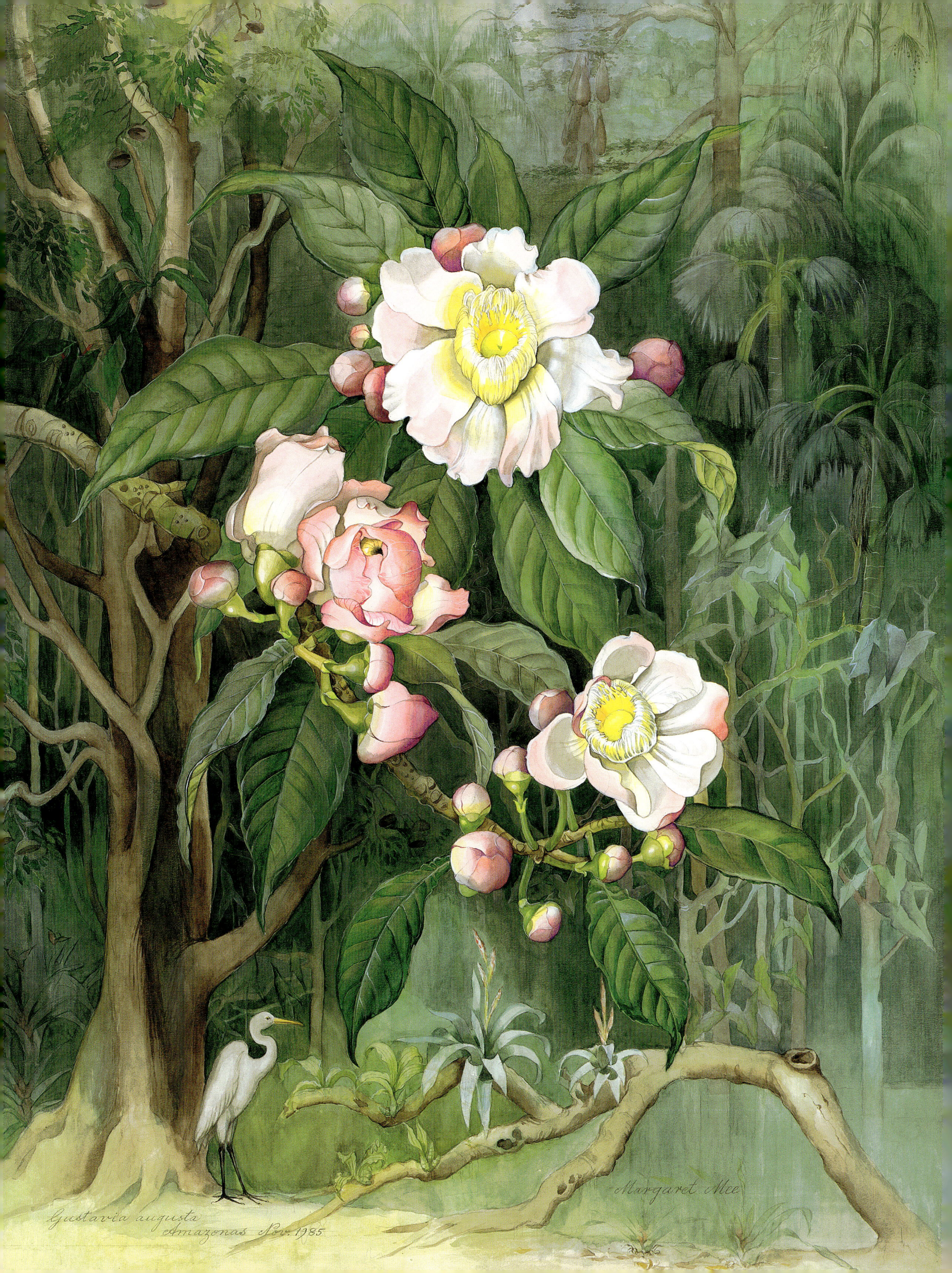
Margaret Mee
Gustavia augusta
Amazonas Nov. 1985

Neoregelia leviana

(family Bromeliaceae)

Pencil and gouache on paper, 1968 (66 x 48.3 cm.)
Collection: Royal Botanic Gardens, Kew

Neoregelia leviana is known scientifically only from Mee's own collection of the species from the banks of the Rio Cauaburi, a left bank tributary of the Rio Negro. She discovered the plant during her attempt to ascend the Pico da Neblina, which lies on the border with Venezuela. Assisted by a scientific grant from the National Geographic Society, Mee became the first woman to attempt a southern approach to this famous mountain. The expedition was abandoned when torrential rains obliterated the path.

Small inlets and igapó *broke the line of forest for almost a hundred miles... As we rounded one bend, a canoe paddled by two young Waika (Yanomami) Indians glided swiftly towards us. They were handsome young men wearing the traditional ornaments of their tribe, two scarlet* arara *tail feathers bound on the upper arm and bunches of parrot feathers in the lobes of their ears. Early in the morning, I found a bromeliad,* Neoregelia leviana, *a very beautiful specimen with fine plants forming a candelabra.*

M. Mee in T. Morrison (ed.), *Margaret Mee: In Search of Flowers of the Amazon Forests*

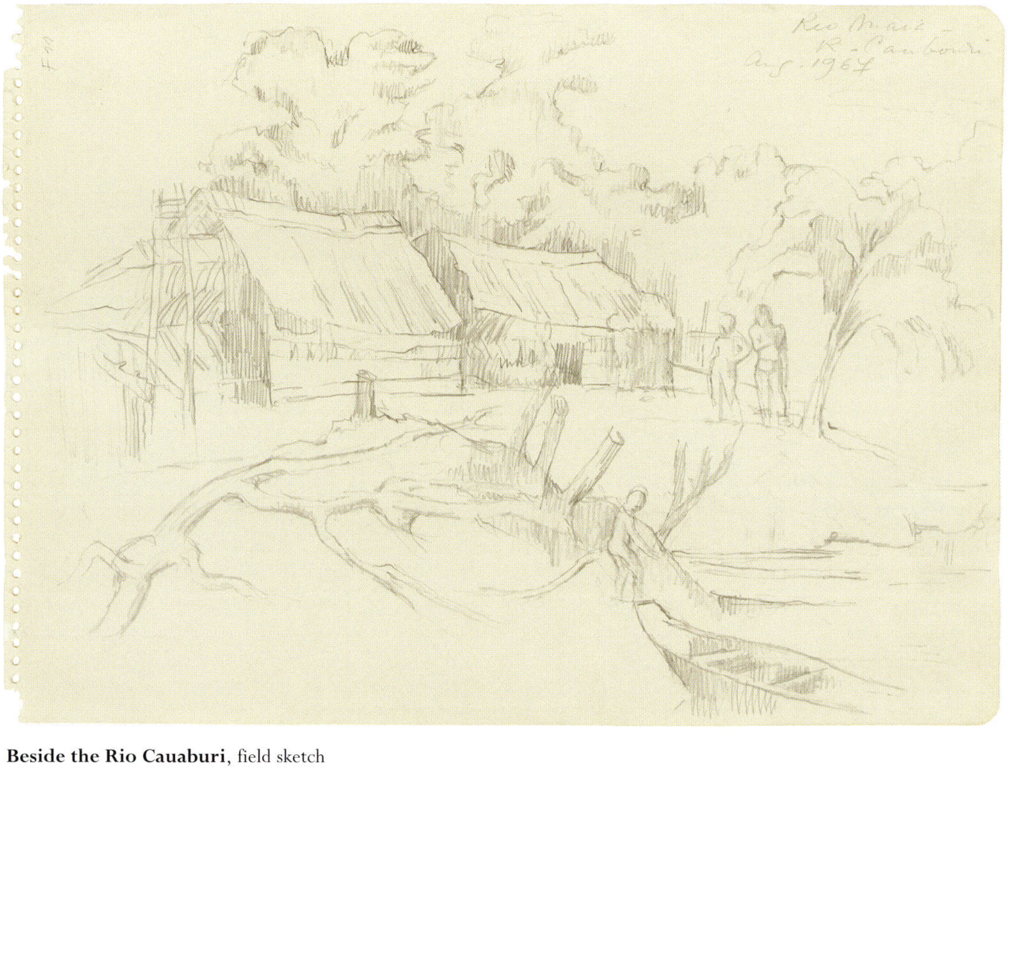

Beside the Rio Cauaburi, field sketch

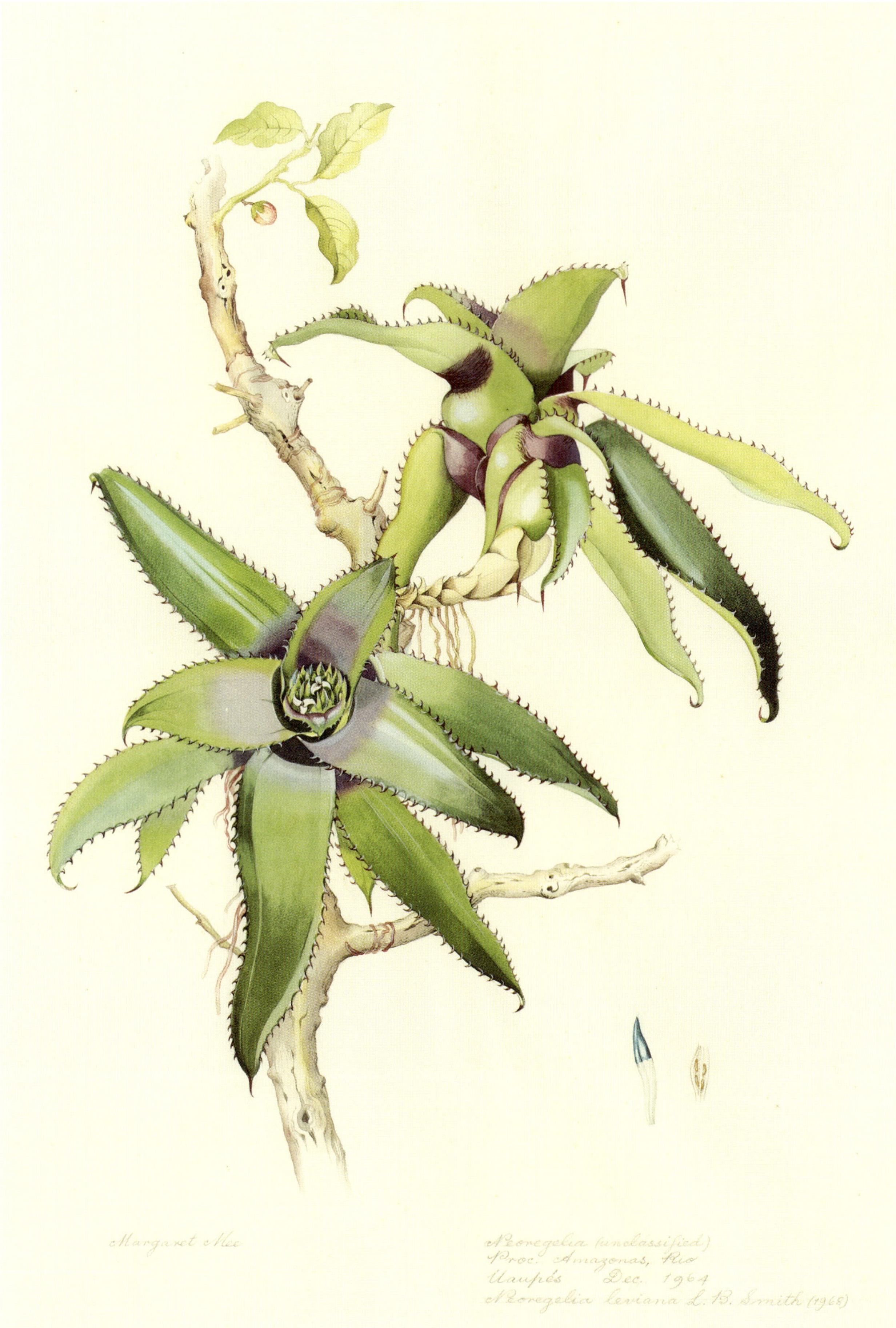
Margaret Mee
Neoregelia (unclassified)
Proc. Amazonas, Rio
Uaupés Dec. 1964
Neoregelia leviana L.B. Smith (1968)

Clusia grandifolia

(family Clusiaceae)

Pencil and gouache on paper, 1982 (73 x 50.8 cm.)
Collection: Royal Botanic Gardens, Kew

In the Amazon region, the common name for the genus *Clusia* is *Rosa da Mata* (Rose of the Forest). Among the plants commonly known as stranglers, *Clusia* seedlings begin life as epiphytes on a host tree. Eventually their aerial roots reach the ground and join laterally. This species was discovered in 1852 by the British explorer, Richard Spruce, who found it in the *igapó* (flooded forest) along the Rio Uaupés, a tributary of the Rio Negro,

Today I made colour sketches of a beautiful Clusia *which I could just reach on the bank, seated in the boat which was rolling in the swell of the river. This is the first time I have seen a perfect specimen of this species… which is a coral colour inside and white outside, looking like a precious piece of porcelain.*

M. Mee in T. Morrison (ed.), *Margaret Mee: In Search of Flowers of the Amazon Forests*

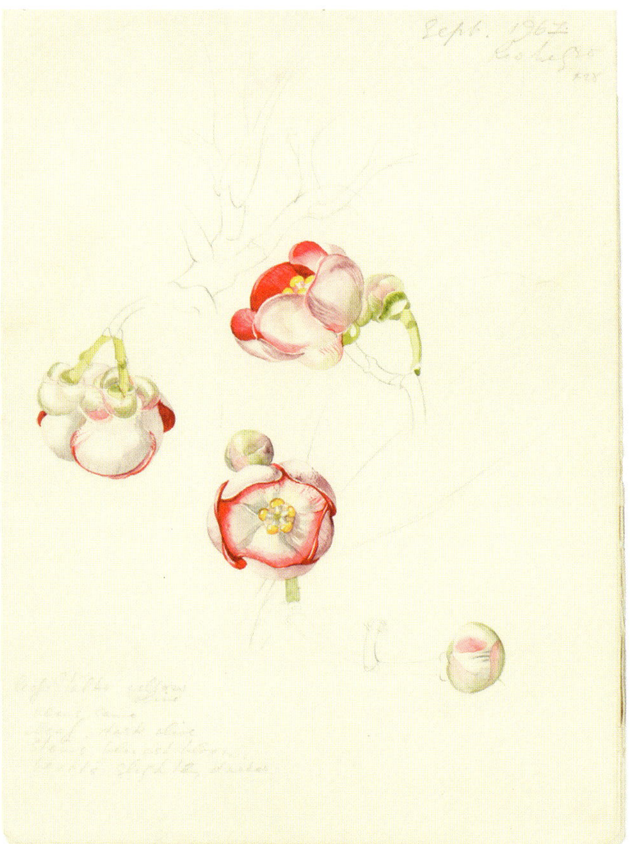

Clusia grandifolia, field sketch

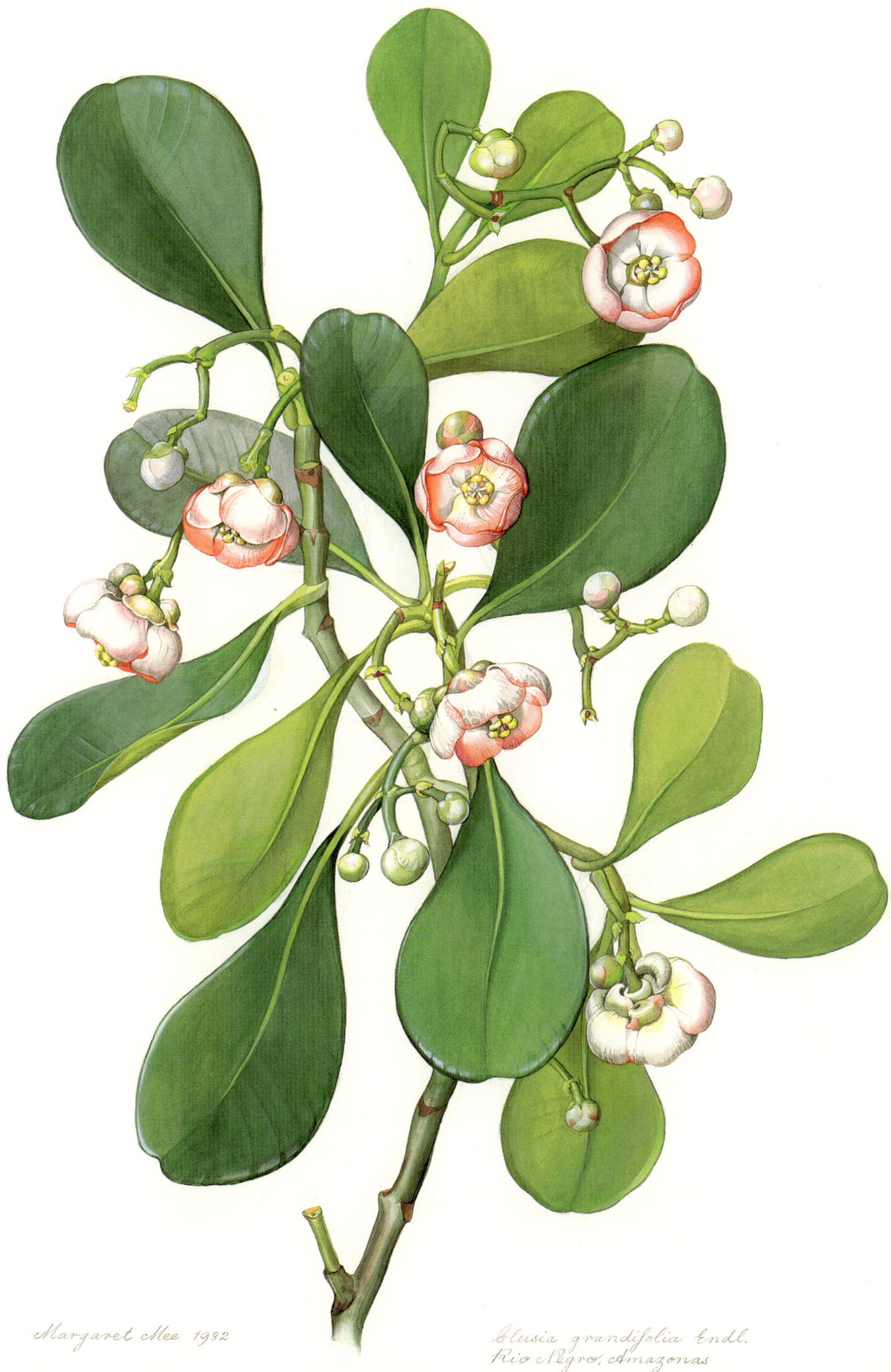
Margaret Mee 1982
Clusia grandifolia Endl.
Rio Negro, Amazonas

Gustavia pulchra

(family Lecythidaceae)

Pencil and gouache on paper, 1979 (65.7 x 47.9 cm.)
Collection: Royal Botanic Gardens, Kew

Gustavia pulchra produces spectacular snow-white flowers up to five inches across. Found in the upper and lower Rio Negro and parts of Venezuela, the tree can reach a height of 60 feet. Born below the leaves, the blooms sprout directly from the branches. This trait, known as cauliflory, is common among rainforest trees. The species was first discovered by the indefatigable nineteenth-century British explorer, Richard Spruce, during his extraordinary journeys throughout Amazonia and the Andes between 1849 and 1864.

Leonardo, my Tariana Indian pilot maneuvered through the waves … We reached the Rio Negro where I found, for the first time, flowers of the magnificent Gustavia pulchra. *There was no time to lose, for the wind was battering the delicate petals as I drew. Will the exquisite beauty of this species save it from extinction?*

M. Mee, *Flowers of the Amazon*

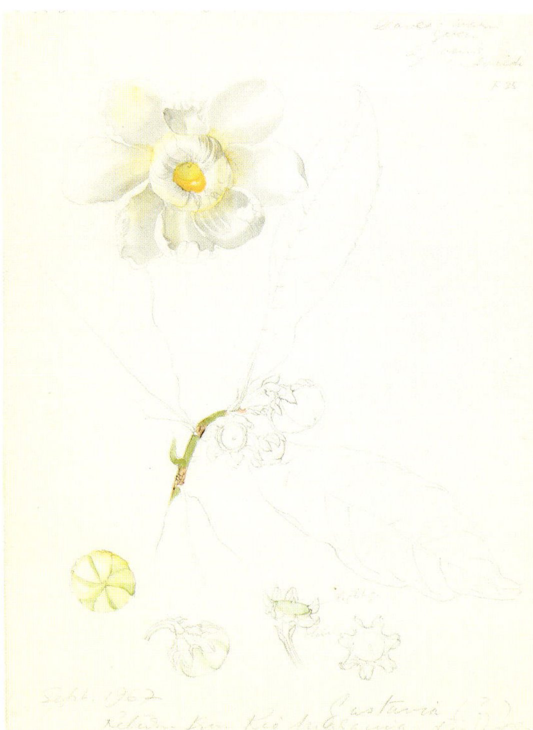

Gustavia pulchra, field sketch

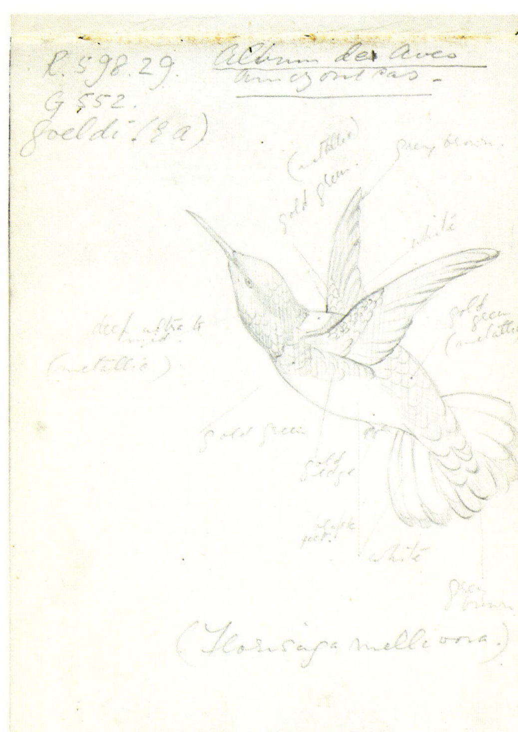

Hummingbird, field sketch

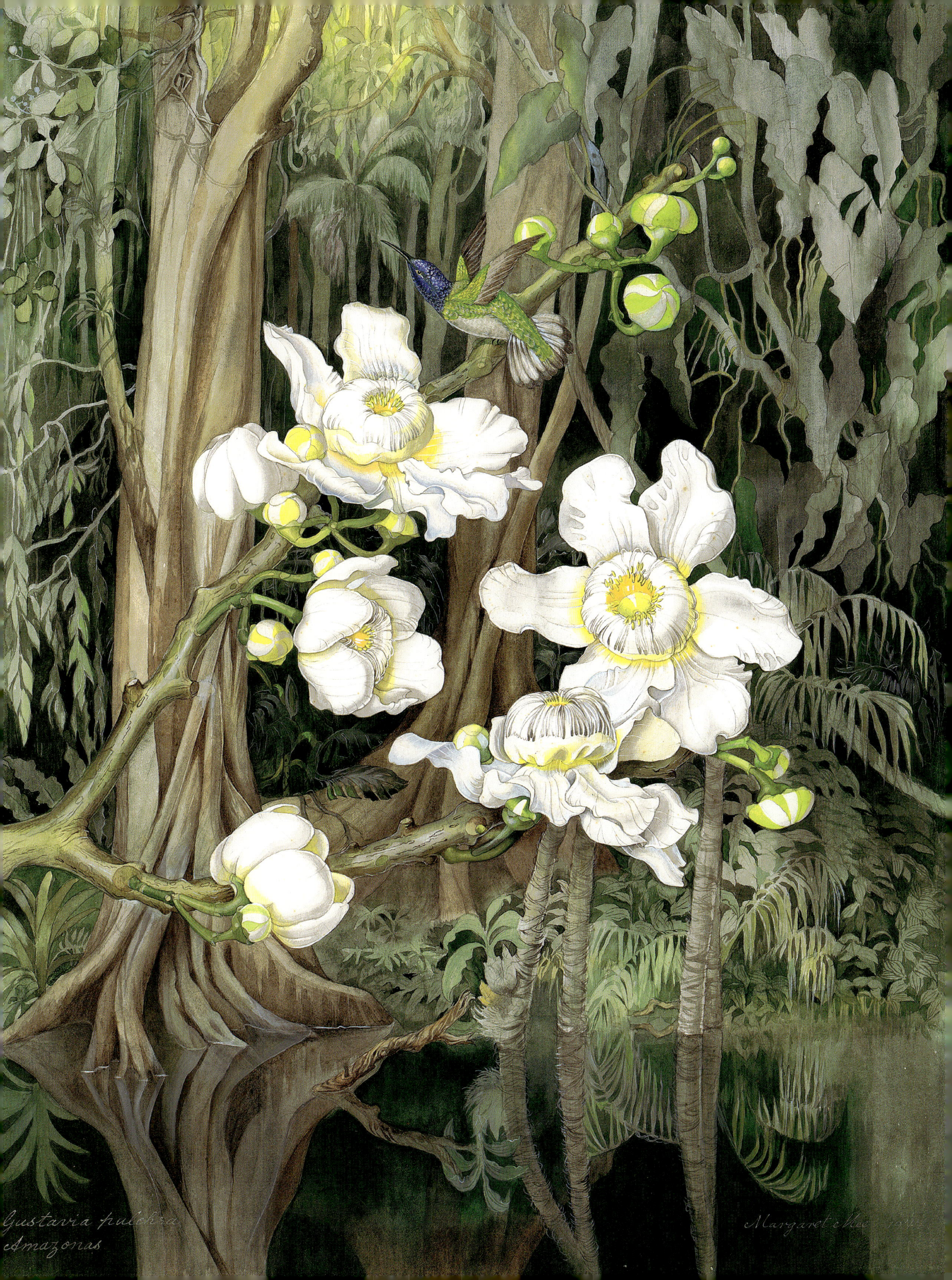
Gustavia pulchra
Amazonas
Margaret Mee

Nymphaea rudgeana

(family Nymphaeaceae)

Pencil and gouache on paper, 1978 (66 x 48.3 cm.)
Collection: Royal Botanic Gardens, Kew

Rarely seen in cultivation, this tropical night-blooming waterlily is a smaller relative of the well-known *Victoria amazonica*, the giant Amazonian waterlily that has, since the last century, remained a coveted show plant of botanic gardens worldwide. *Nymphaea rudgeana* was first discovered by the intrepid British explorer, Richard Spruce, in 1849. The flowers reportedly open at dusk, emitting a lemon scent that attracts its pollinator, a scarab beetle.

Does this beautiful lake where I found Nymphaea rudgeana *in flower still exist? They were putting the surrounding primary forest to axe and fire … I hope that the enormous Black* Onça *(jaguar) of Indian legends dwells at the bottom of the lake to protect it from the ravages of man.*

M. Mee, *Flowers of the Amazon*

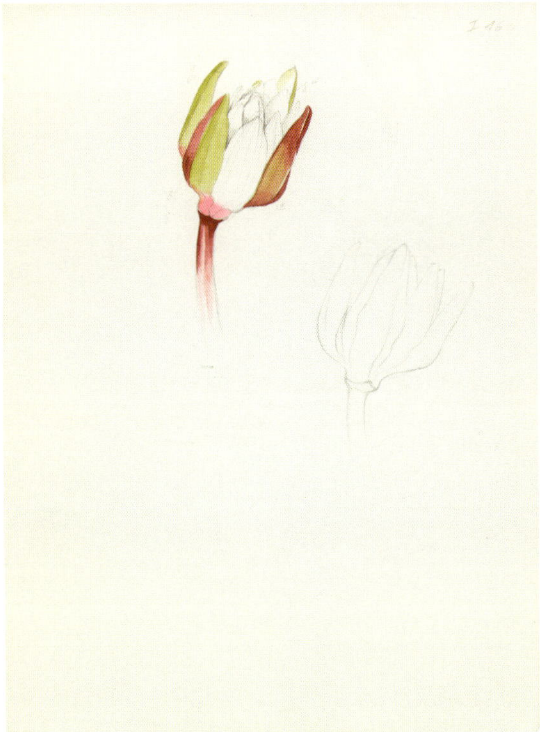

Nymphaea rudgeana, field sketch

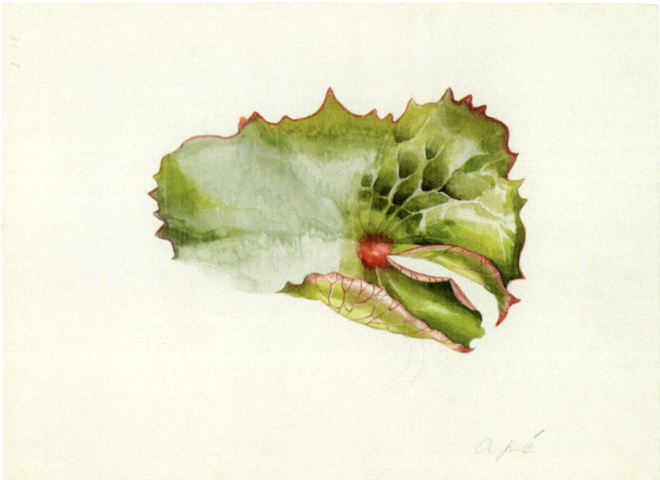

Nymphaea rudgeana, field sketch

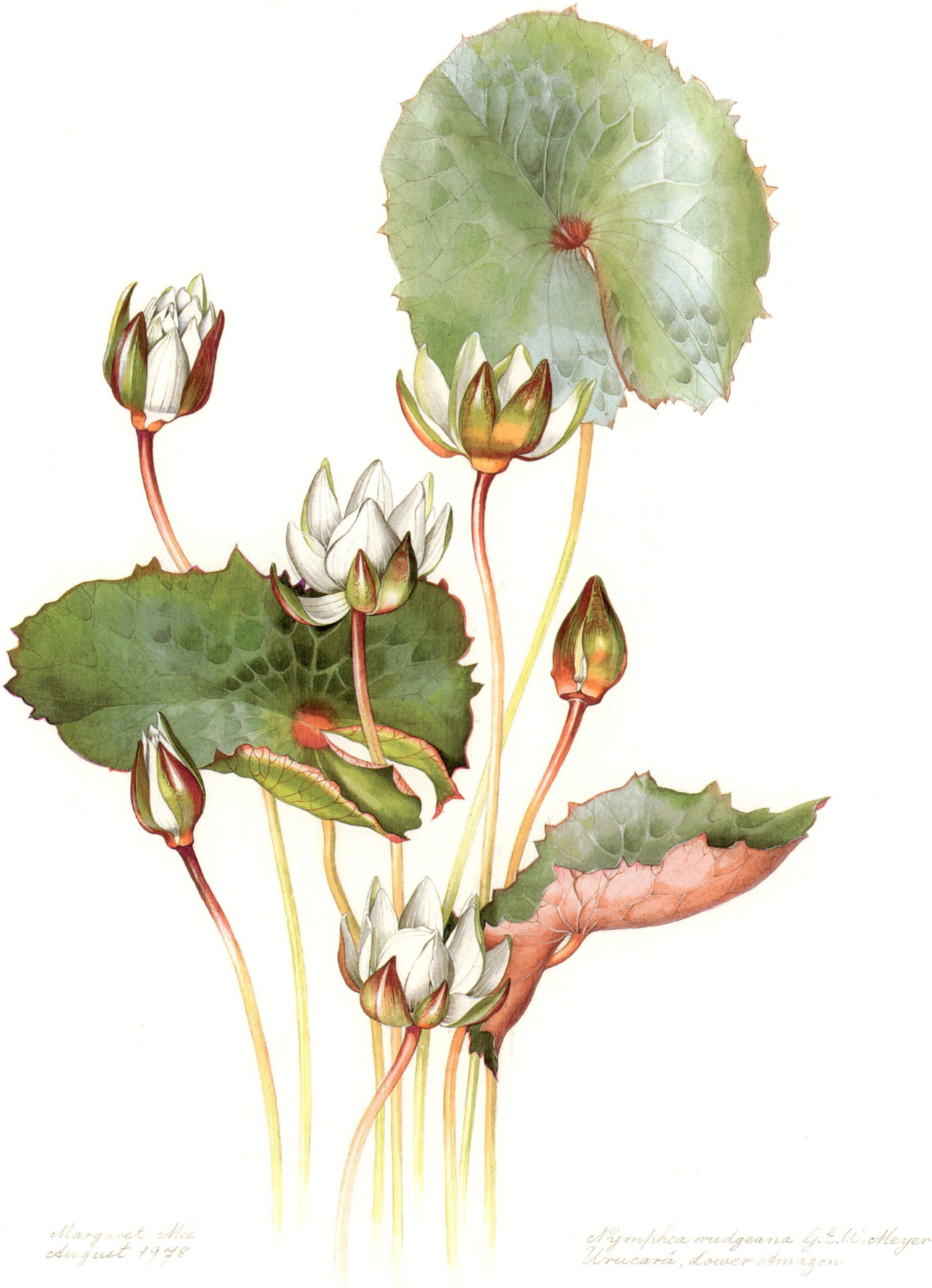
Margaret Mee
August 1978
Nymphea rudgeana G.E.W. Meyer
Urucará, Lower Amazon

Aechmea rodriguesiana

(family Bromeliaceae)

Pencil and gouache on paper, 1977 (65.7 x 47.9 cm.)
Collection: Royal Botanic Gardens, Kew

Aechmea rodriguesiana was named in honour of William A. Rodrigues, the notable Brazilian botanist who first discovered it in the area of the Ducke Reserve near Manaus. The plant grows epiphytically in the region of the lower Amazon and Rio Negro. Mee depicted it within its rainforest habitat, inserting a twig from a young *Clusia* epiphyte and, in the background, the curious leaves of the aroid *Philodendron goeldii*.

I caught sight of a large bromeliad ... The flowers were dry and the fruit already forming. As this was a species I had never seen before, I decided to return to the area again in the flowering season. About six months later, I found Aechmea rodriguesiana *again – this time in full flower, the rose pink bracts enclosing pure white florets.*

M. Mee, *Flowers of the Amazon*

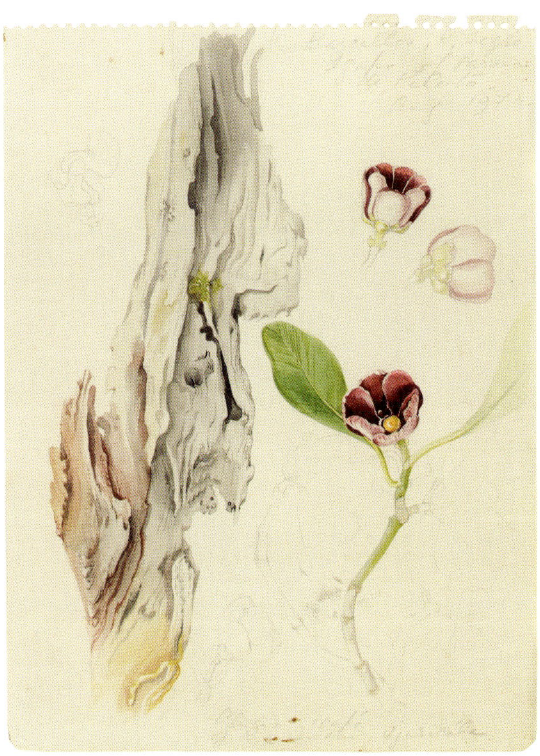

***Clusia* and weathered wood,** field sketch

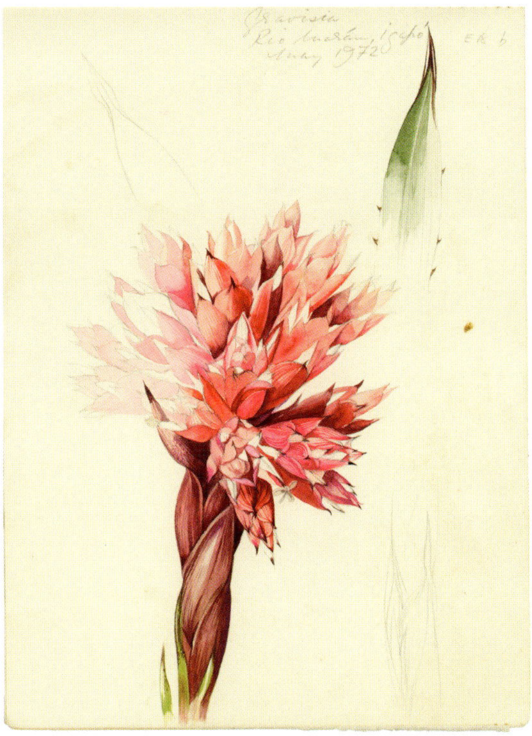

Aechmea rodriguesiana, field sketch

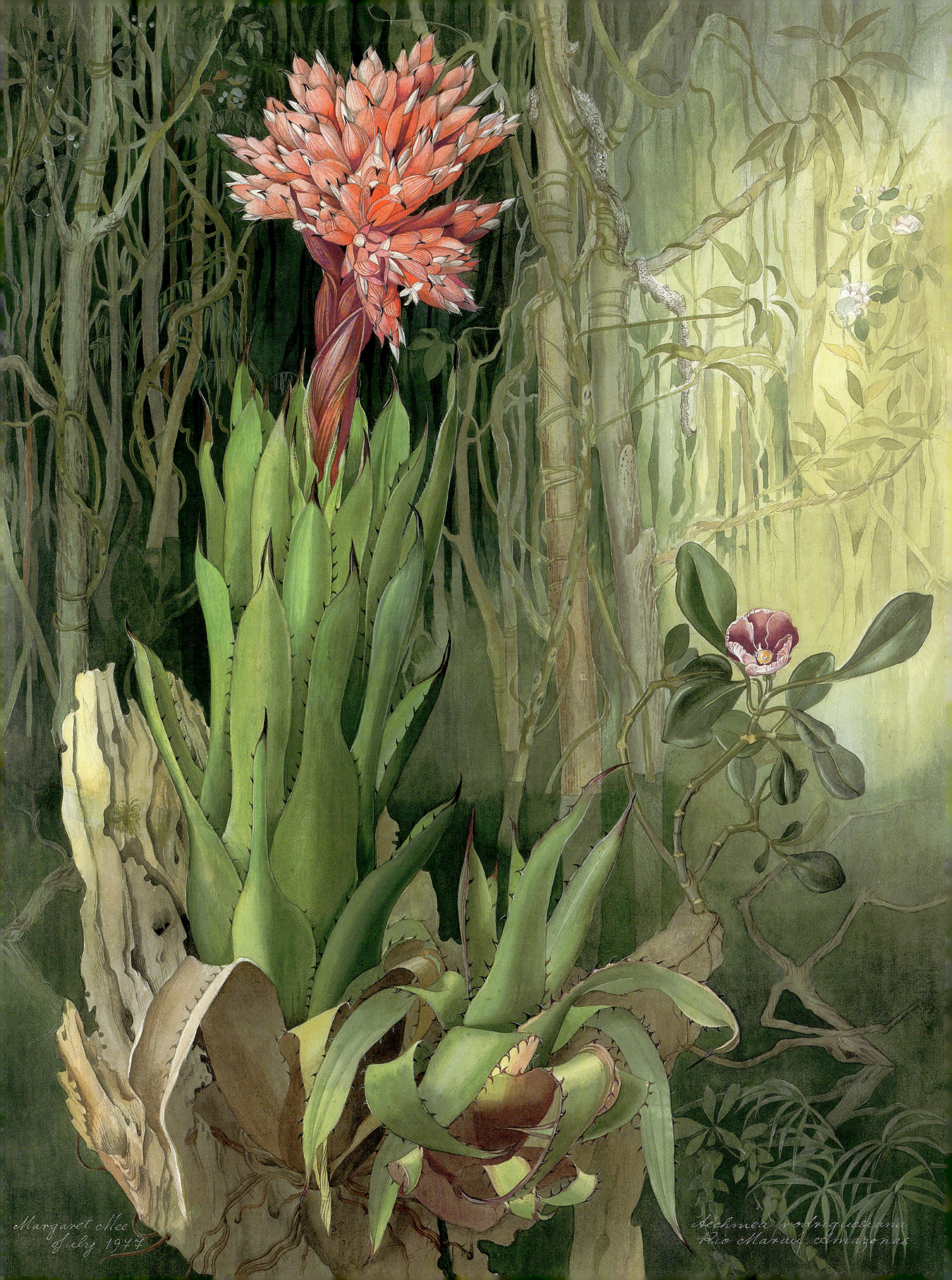
Margaret Mee
July 1977
Aechmea rodriguesiana
Rio Maraú, Amazonas

Rudolfiella aurantiaca

(family Orchidaceae)

Pencil and gouache on paper, 1971 (66 x 47.9 cm.)
Collection: Royal Botanic Gardens, Kew

The inflorescences of this striking plant bear up to twenty, golden yellow, red-spotted flowers. Here Mee depicts the plant as she observed it, perched on a *Jará* palm in the flooded forests of the Rio Negro, a common habitat for this epiphytic orchid. It is widely distributed in the Amazonian area of Brazil, Peru, Colombia, Venezuela, and the Guianas.

Orchids grow in profusion on the stems of the Jará *palms, weaving their roots into the fibrous bark. It was on such a palm that I found* Rudolfiella aurantiaca *... I made some drawings and colour notes, seated in the boat, fearing that the delicate flowers would not weather the return journey.*

M. Mee, *Flowers of the Amazon*

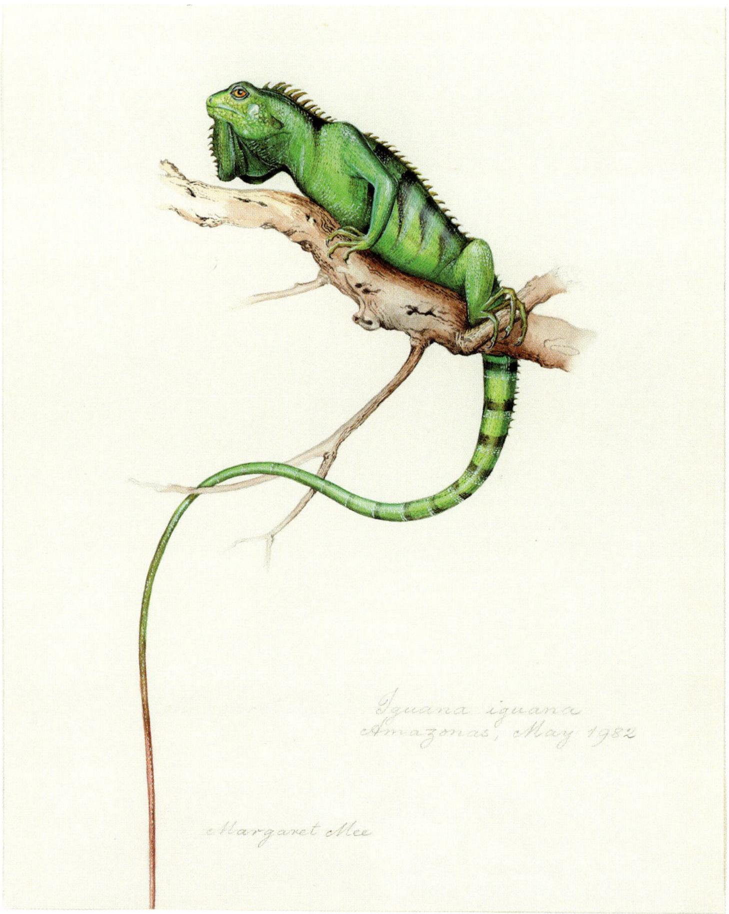

Iguana, field study (Collection: Greville Mee)

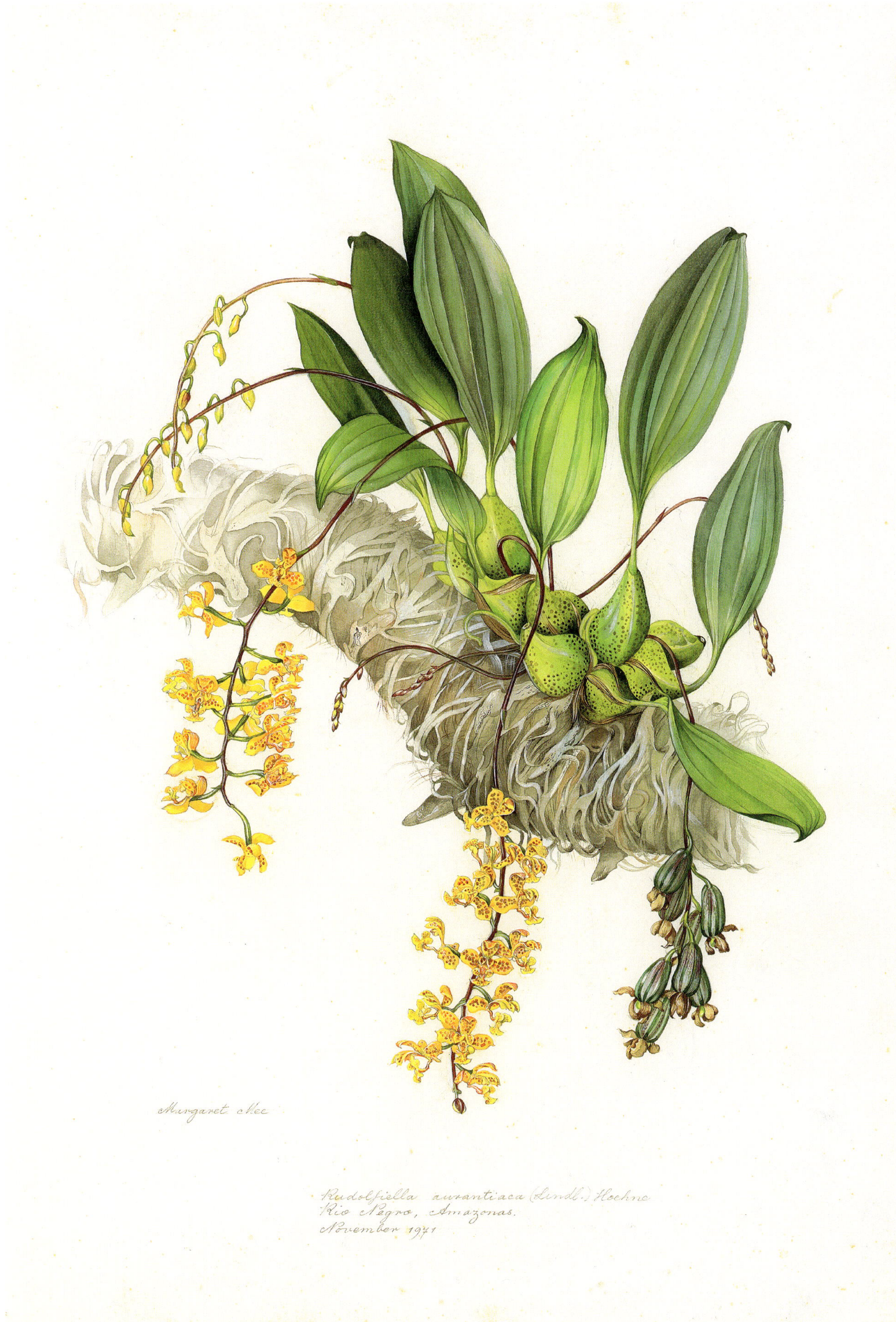
Margaret Mee
Rudolfiella aurantiaca (Lindl.) Hoehne
Rio Negro, Amazonas.
November 1971

Oncidium lanceanum

(family Orchidaceae)

Pencil and gouache on paper, 1975 (65.7 x 47.9 cm.)
Collection: Royal Botanic Gardens, Kew

As a member of the so-called 'Mule-ear' orchids, this plant is distinctive for its erect, leathery leaves, finely mottled with red to chocolate-brown colouring. The genus *Oncidium* contains more than 400 species of epiphytes and remains one of the most widely cultivated and popular genera. Collected along the banks of the upper Rio Negro, this orchid bears long-lasting, intensely fragrant flowers, whose scent is reminiscent of cloves.

On the day before returning, I found Oncidium lanceanum *in the great* macucuzinho *tree, but without flowers ... In the* igapó *we passed under the discarded skin of a large snake, hanging from the trees like a gossamer liana.*

M. Mee, *Flowers of the Amazon*

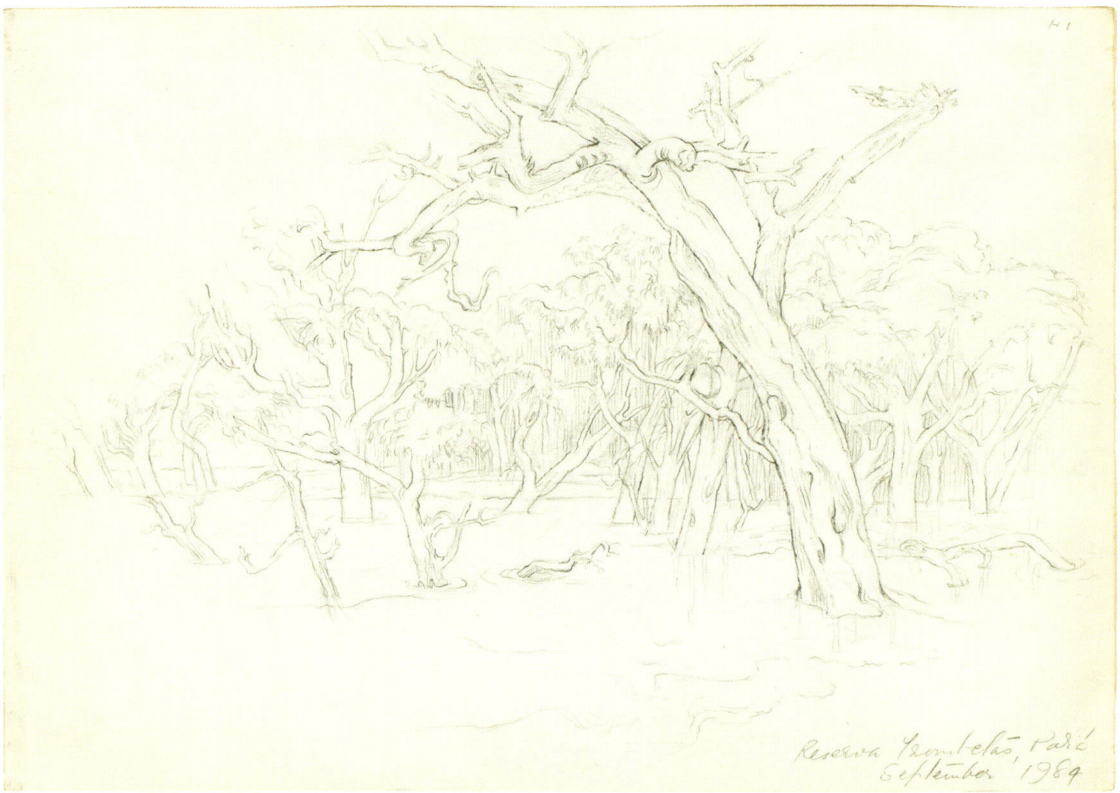

Igapó, field sketch

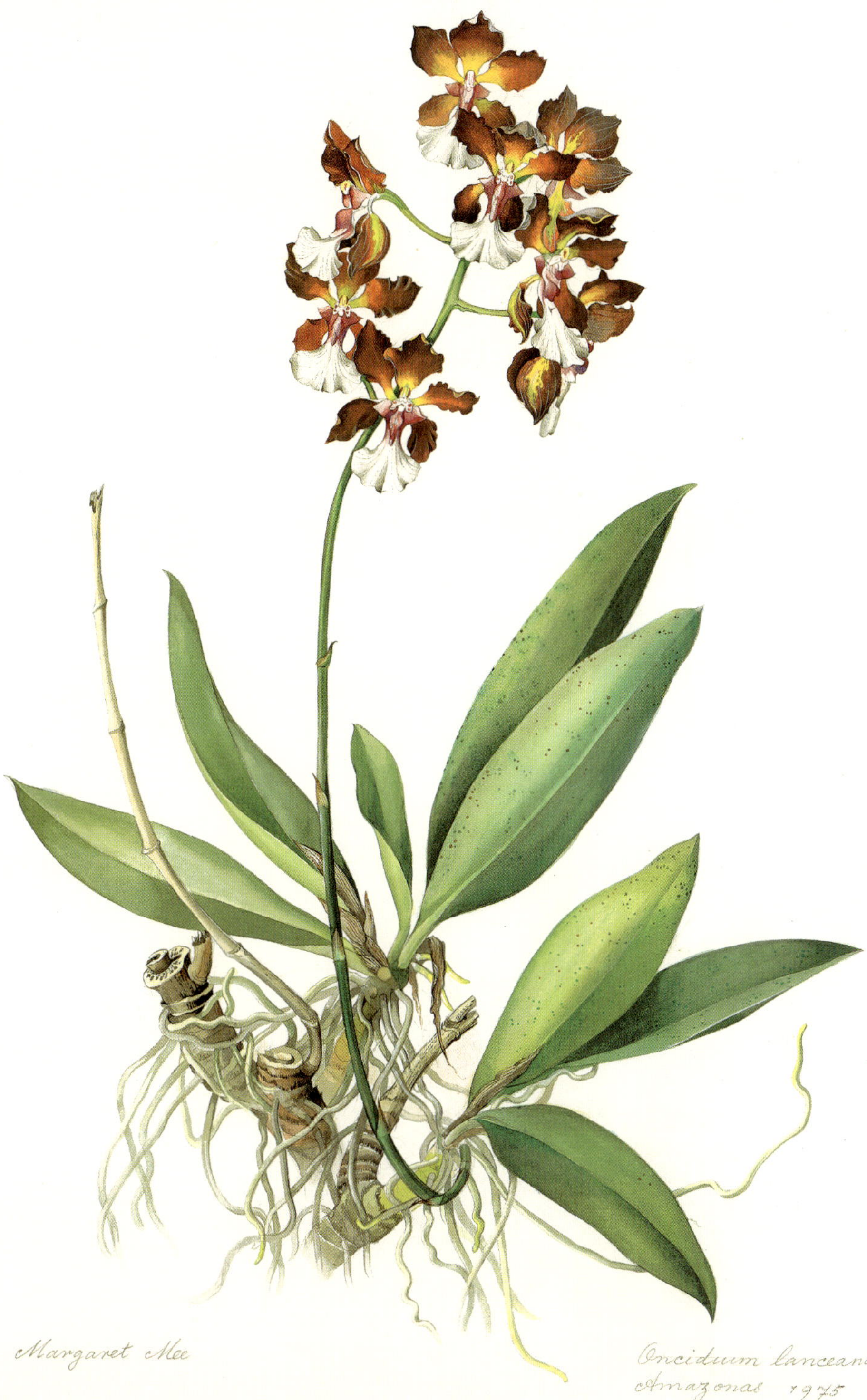
Margaret Mee
Oncidium lanceana Lindl.
Amazonas 1975

Cattleya violacea

(family Orchidaceae)

Pencil and gouache on paper, 1981 (66 x 48.3 cm.)
Collection: Royal Botanic Gardens, Kew

The genus *Cattleya* is one of the most widely grown genera in the orchid family. These plants were first introduced into England in 1818, arriving in a crate from Brazil with the leaves of *Cattleya* orchids serving as a protective outer wrapping for lichens and mosses. William Cattley, the notable British horticulturist, recognized the plants as unusual and nurtured them until they flowered in 1824.

Cattleya violacea was first discovered on the Rio Orinoco in Venezuela by Alexander von Humboldt and his companion Aimé Bonpland during their celebrated journey to the Americas between 1799 and 1804.

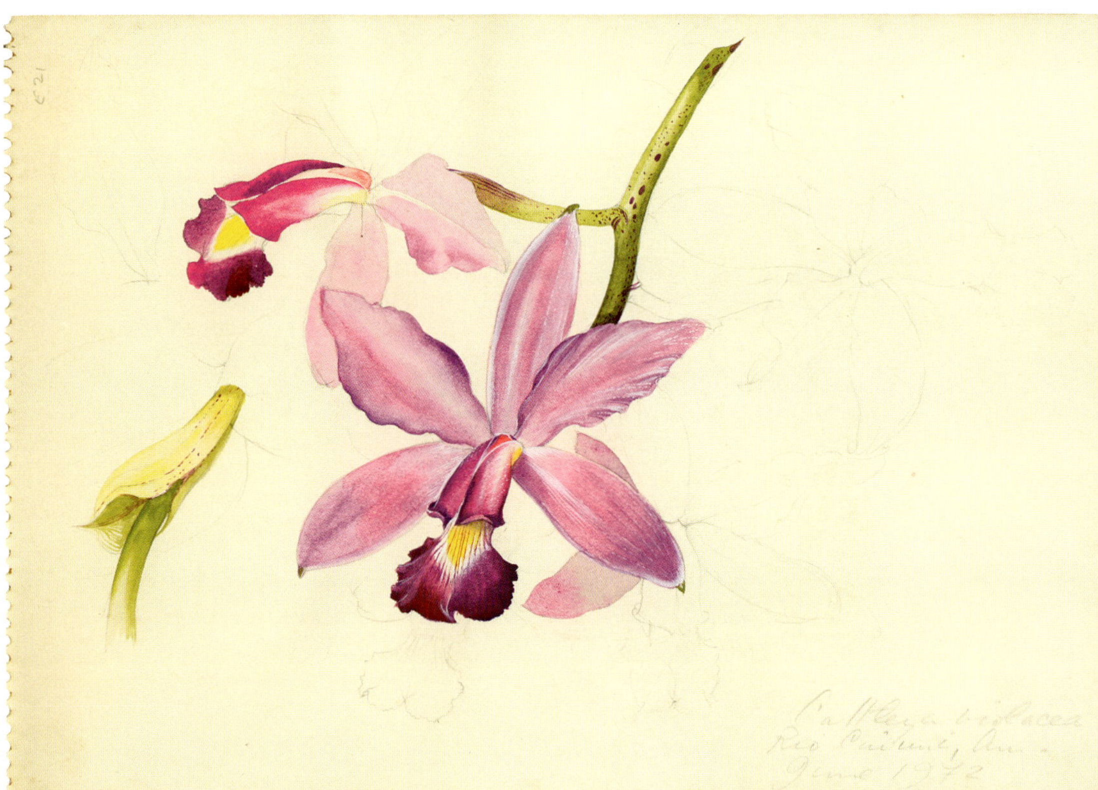

Cattleya violacea, field sketch

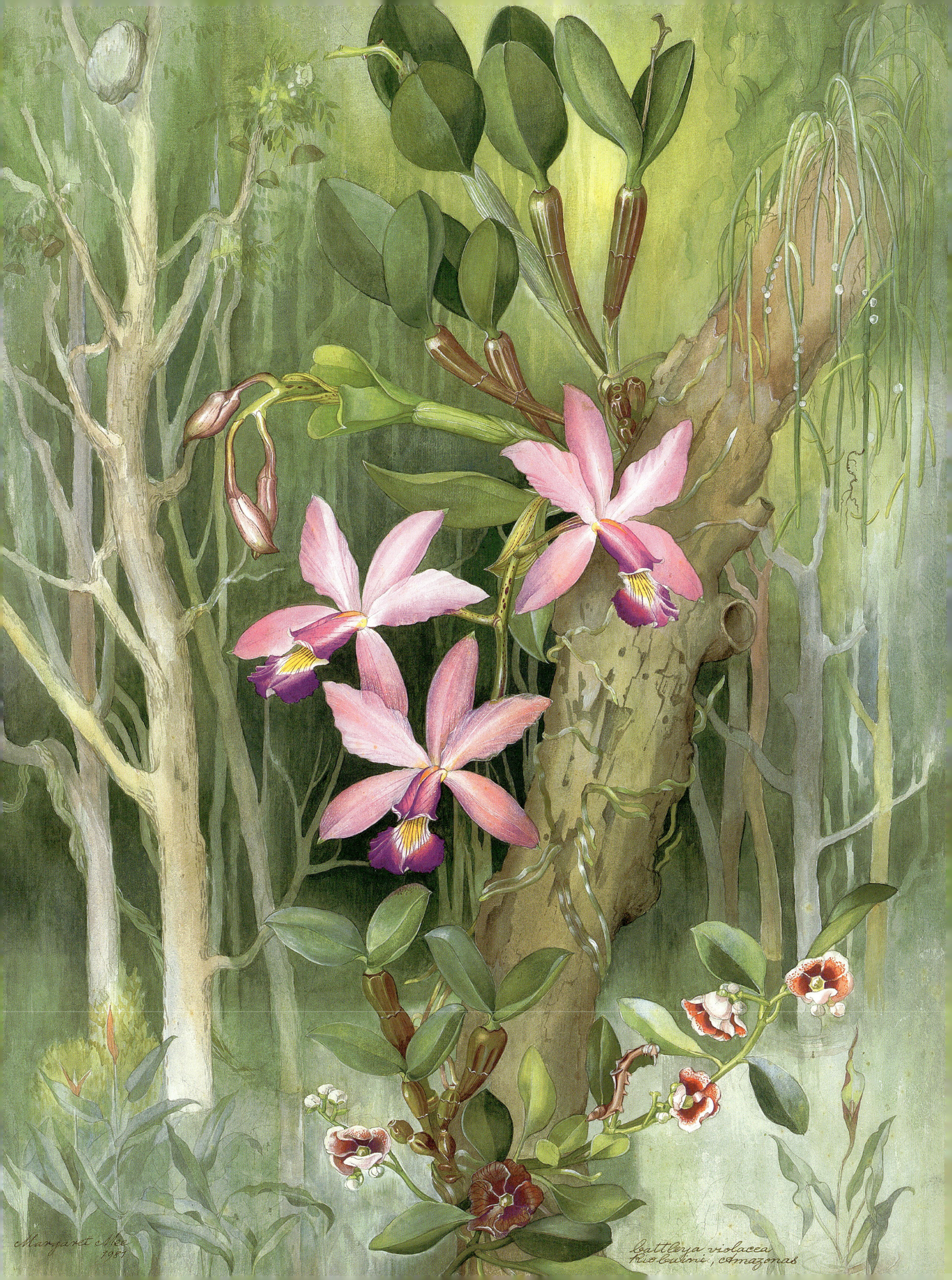
Margaret Mee
1981
Cattleya violacea
Rio Cuini, Amazonas

Streptocalyx poeppigii

(family Bromeliaceae)

Pencil and gouache on paper, 1985 (71.8 x 50.5 cm.)
Collection: Royal Botanic Gardens, Kew

Streptocalyx poeppigii, distributed widely throughout Colombia, Amazonian Brazil, eastern Peru and Bolivia, was collected by and named for the nineteenth-century German botanist and explorer, Eduard Poeppig, who made a significant early expedition to both Peru and Brazil. *S. poeppigii* grows epiphytically in the rainforest. Its robust inflorescence, with rose-purple flowers, is replaced by pink and white berries that gradually turn purple in colour and remain for months.

Margaret Mee was deeply troubled by the growing threats to the Amazon. By including the forest background in paintings such as this one, she emphasized the interdependency of forest species and the importance of preserving their habitats. Note the *Nymphaea* plants in the lower right corner of the painting.

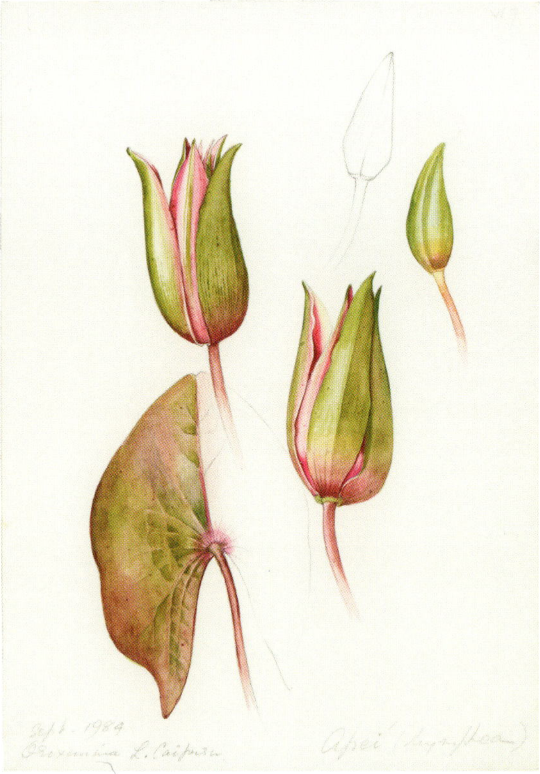

***Nymphaea* sp.**, field sketch

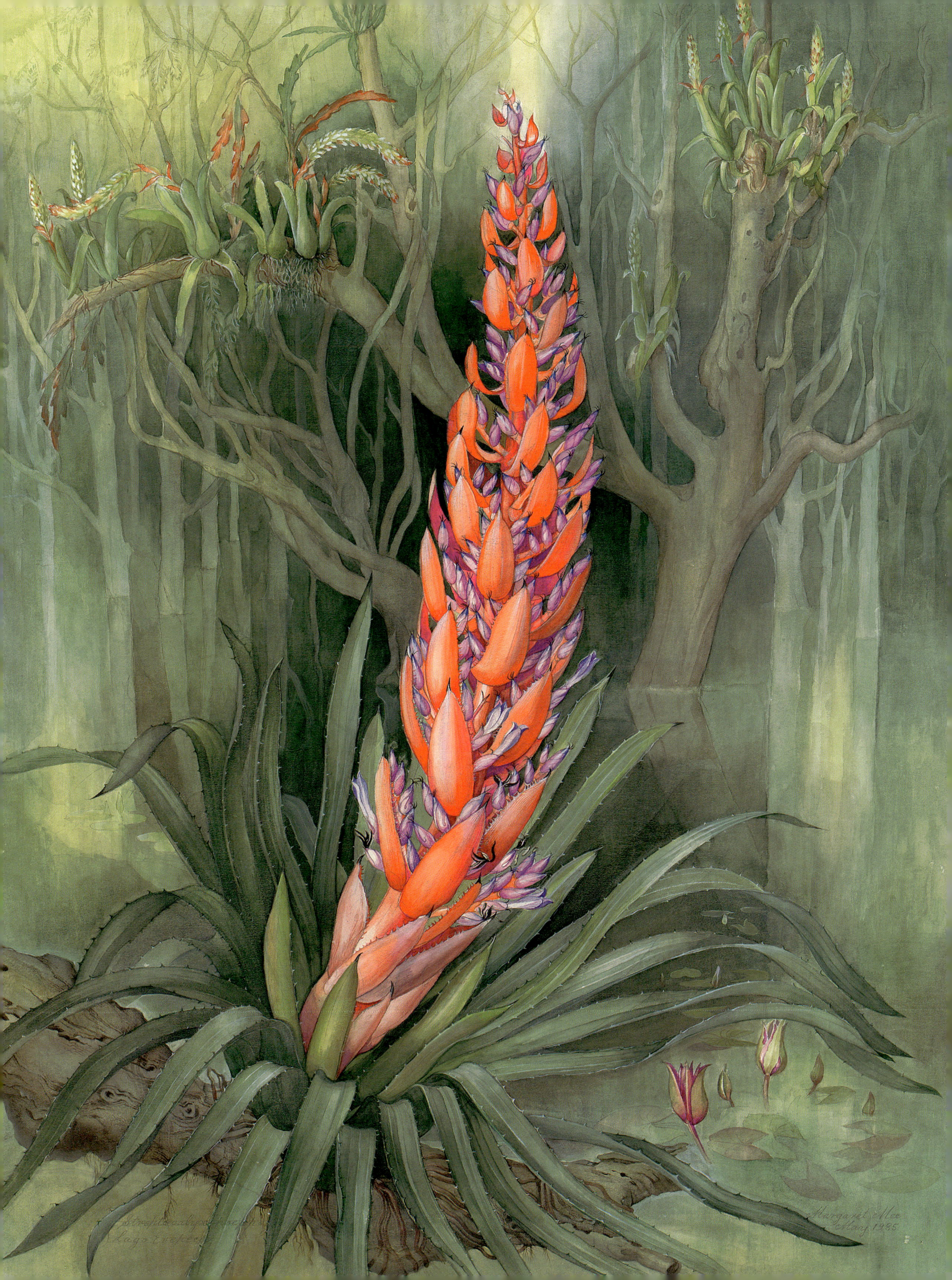
Margaret Mee
May 1985

Selenicereus wittii

(family Cactaceae)

Pencil and gouache on paper, 1978 (66 x 48.3 cm.)
Collection: Royal Botanic Gardens, Kew

Having first seen the epiphytic cactus *Selenicereus wittii* on her third journey, in 1964, Margaret Mee was determined to paint the elusive 'Moonflower' in full bloom within its natural habitat of the *igapó*. Her pursuit would continue for twenty-four years, during which time she was fortunate enough to locate this rare plant on three different occasions.

In this painting, Mee's first of the species, *Selenicereus wittii* is portrayed within its forest surroundings, depicting its developing fruits and curious, spine-edged flattened stems, suffused with crimson.

This strange cactus has its roots on the underside of the leaf; thus it clings close to the bark of the tree and appears almost like a design in low relief.

M. Mee in T. Morrison (ed.), *Margaret Mee: In Search of Flowers of the Amazon Forests*

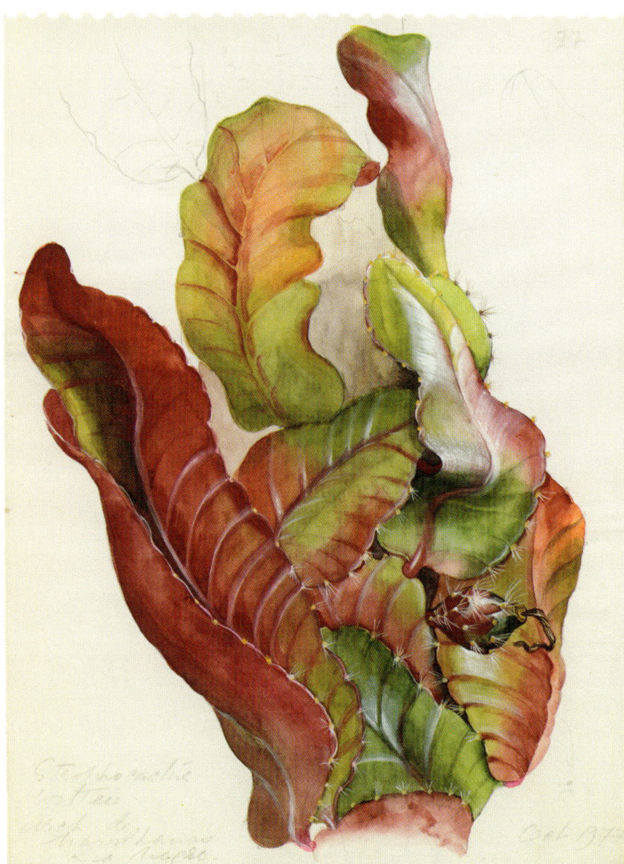

Selenicereus wittii, field sketch

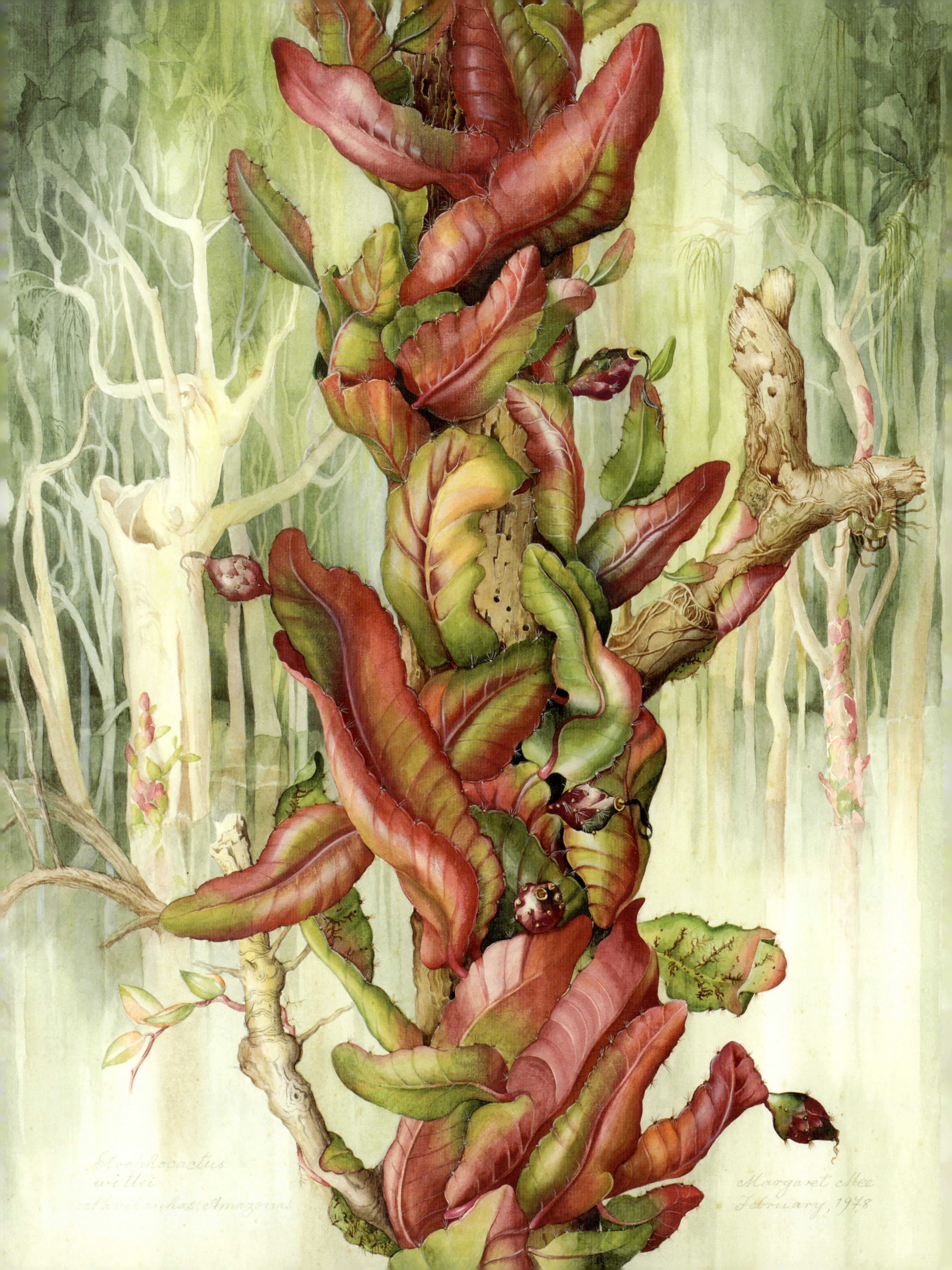
Strophocactus
wittei
Paulinhas, Amazonas
Margaret Mee
February, 1978

Selenicereus wittii

(family Cactaceae)

Pencil and gouache on paper, 1981 (66 x 48.3 cm.)
Collection: Royal Botanic Gardens, Kew

Each flower of *Selenicereus wittii* has the form of a very long tube which splays out rather abruptly at the tip. This shape, combined with the night-flowering habit, suggests that pollination is by long-tongued hawkmoths. Mee noted this rare cactus during her earlier expeditions, but always without flowers. This painting portrays plants that had bloomed the previous night.

The flower had opened and closed overnight ... one brief night of glorious show. Flowering was over, and all I could do was to think of searching again in another year.

M. Mee in T. Morrison (ed.), *Margaret Mee: In Search of Flowers of the Amazon Forests*

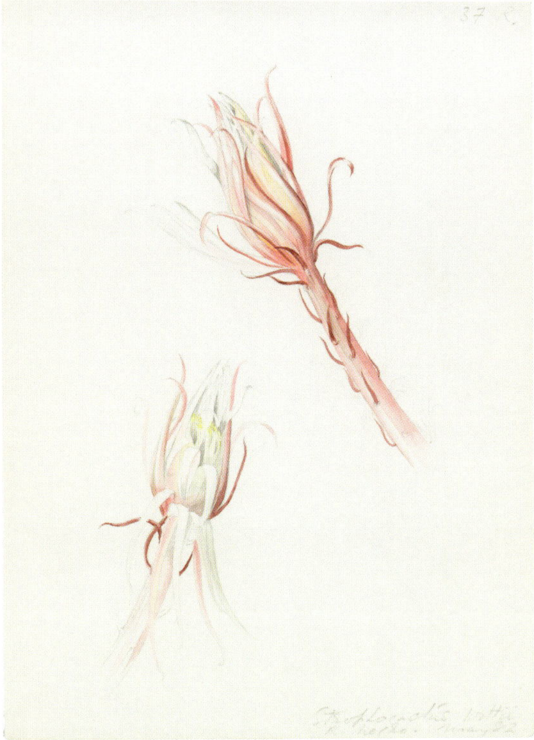

Selenicereus wittii, field sketch

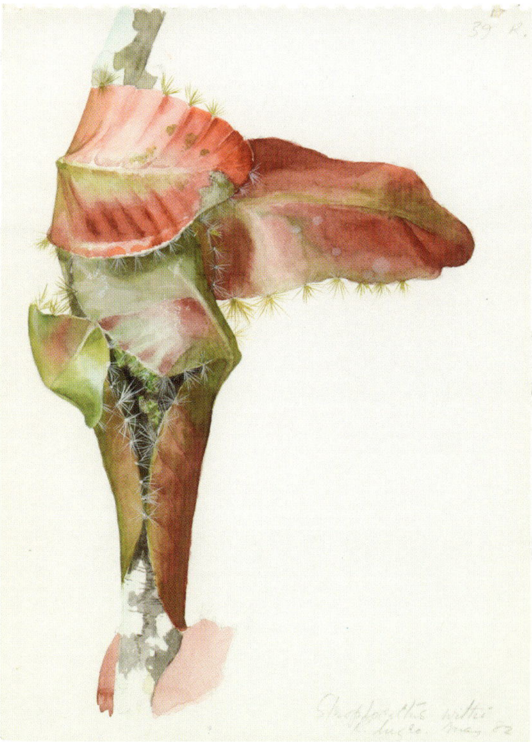

Selenicereus wittii, field sketch

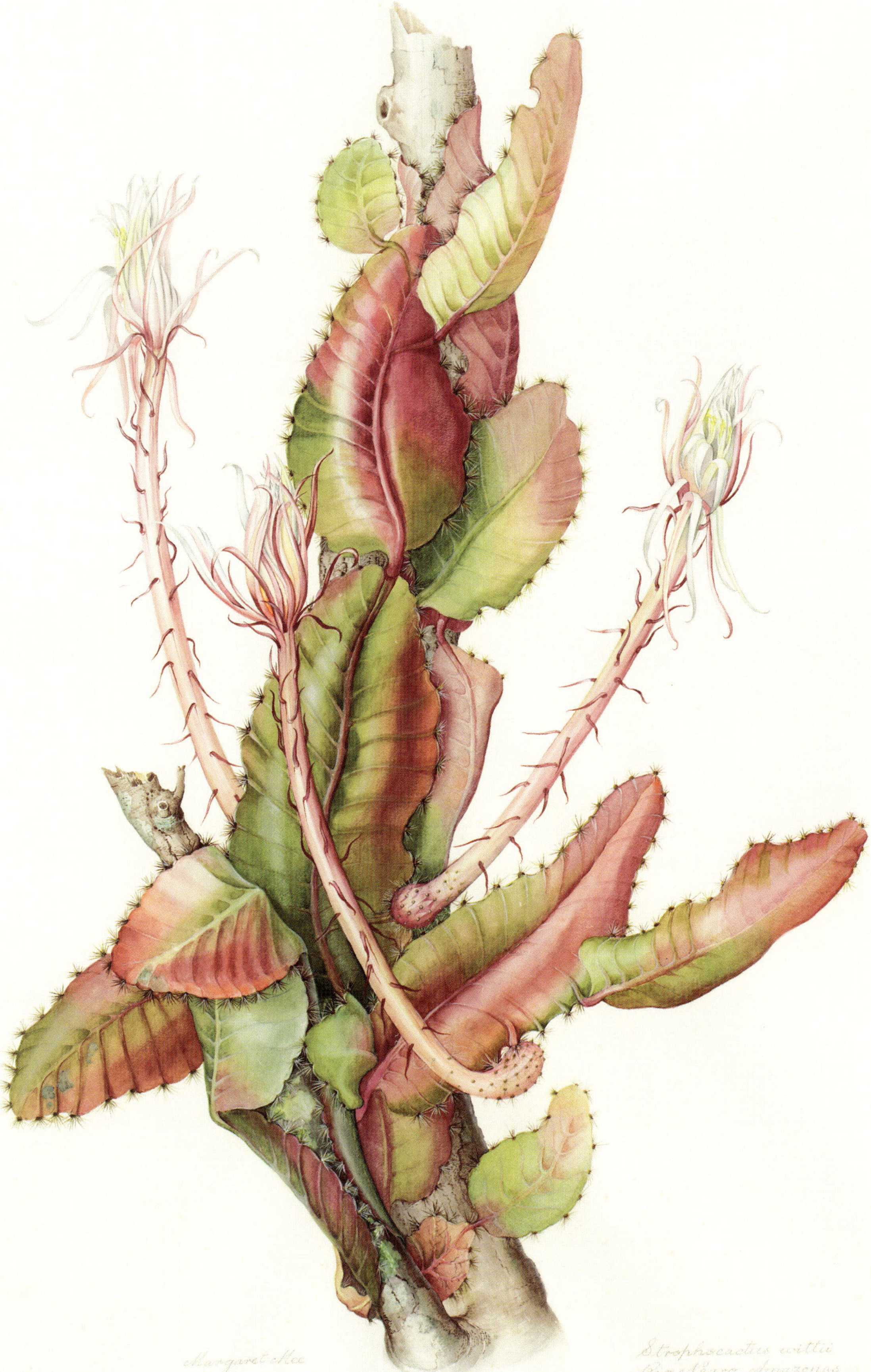
Margaret Mee
Strophocactus wittii
Rio Negro, Amazonas

Selenicereus wittii

(family Cactaceae)

Pencil and gouache on paper, 1988 (66 x 48.3 cm.)
Collection: Greville Mee

The striking bloom of *Selenicereus wittii* opens at night and lasts only until dawn. It is related to the 'Queen of the Night,' *Selenicereus grandiflorus*, a widely cultivated plant perhaps best known from Robert Thornton's magnificent folio, *The Temple of Flora*, published 1797-1807. The generic name is derived from the Greek *selene*, meaning moon.

During an all-night vigil in May 1988, Margaret Mee witnessed the ephemeral blossoming of the 'Moonflower' cactus, thus realizing a long cherished dream. It was the month of her 79th birthday and barely six months before her tragic death. Mee sketched the plant by torchlight from the deck of a riverboat along the banks of the Rio Negro, a triumph that crowned her career as a botanical artist.

In the early stages an extraordinarily sweet perfume wafted from the flower, and we were all transfixed by the beauty of the delicate and unexpectedly large bloom, fully open in an hour... With the dawn the flower closed, and we watched fascinated and humbled by the experience.

M. Mee in T. Morrison (ed.), *Margaret Mee: In Search of Flowers of the Amazon Forests*

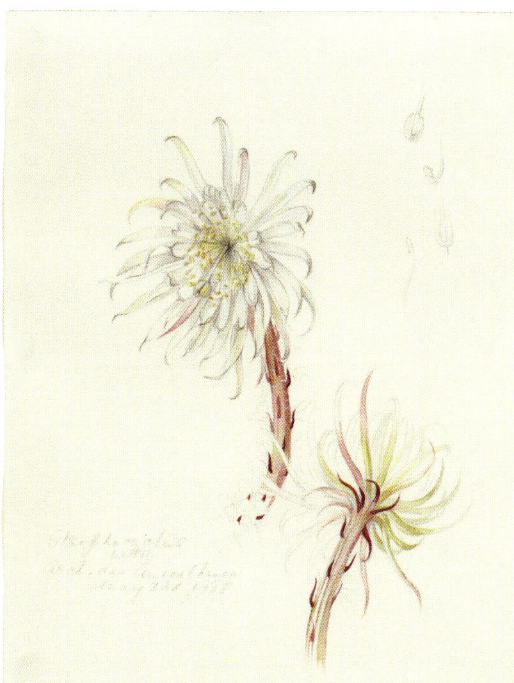

Selenicereus wittii, field sketch

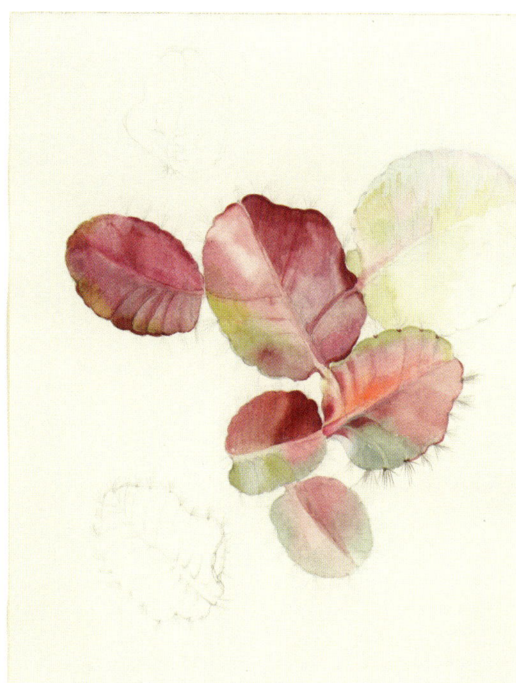

Selenicereus wittii, field sketch

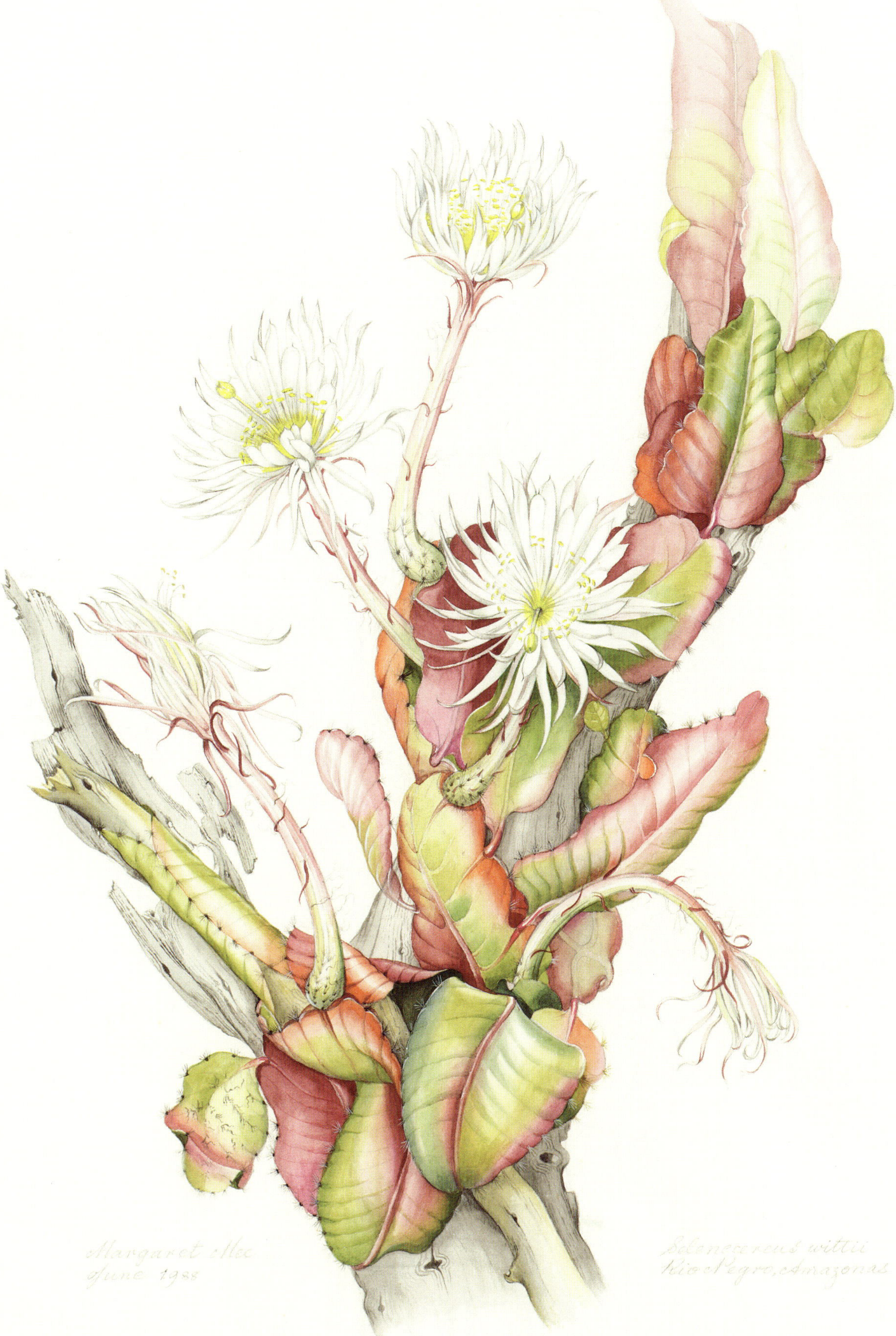
Margaret Mee
June 1988
Selenicereus wittii
Rio Negro, Amazonas

Neoregelia margaretae

(family Bromeliaceae)

Pencil and gouache on paper, 1979 (66 x 48.3 cm.)
Collection: Royal Botanic Gardens, Kew

Margaret Mee collected four of the five species of *Neoregelia* known from Amazonian Brazil, and is credited with first discovering three of them – *N. margaretae, N. leviana,* and *N. meeana*. Mee's contribution to the knowledge of this genus helped establish her reputation as both a scientist and a botanical explorer. As *Neoregelia margaretae* has not yet been recollected, it is known only from Mee's collections.

The painting accurately depicts the splendour of *N. margaretae*. At its centre are tiny blue and white flowers set in a sunken cluster and surrounded by the brilliant, rose-coloured inner leaves of the rosette. The reservoir formed by the leaves of the plant becomes filled with rainwater, providing a home for a myriad of animal life, from tiny insects to small vertebrates such as frogs or lizards. When these animals die, their bodies provide nutrition for the plant.

During the months of heavy rainfall in Içana, the forests there will be studded with these magenta jewels.

M. Mee, *Flowers of the Brazilian Forest*

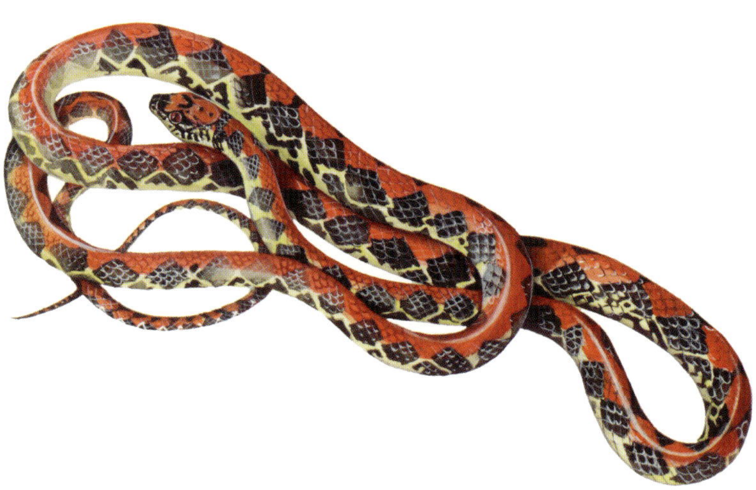

Coral Snake, field study (Collection: Greville Mee)

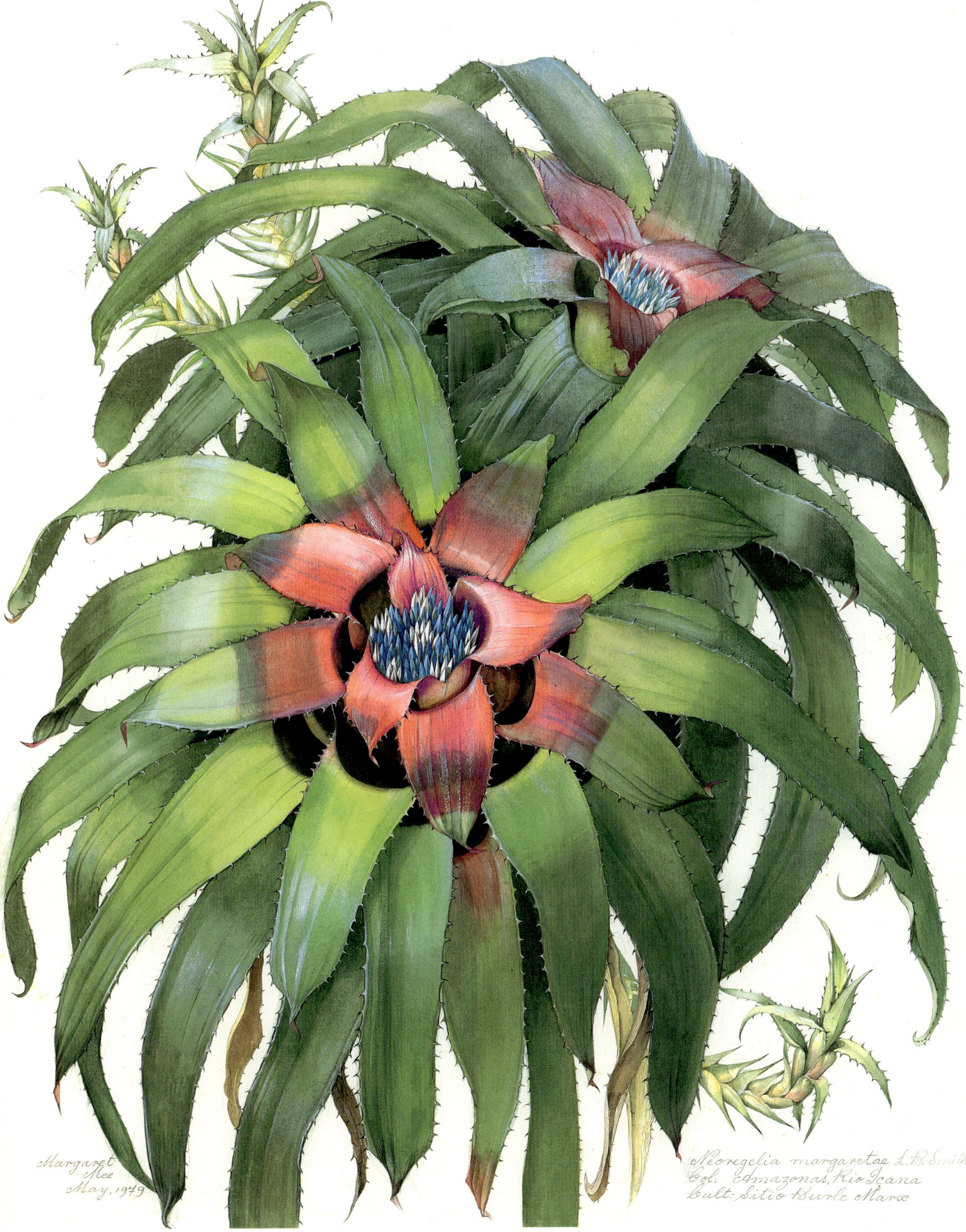
Margaret
Mee
May, 1979
Neoregelia margaretae L.B. Smith
Col: Amazonas, Rio Içana
Cult: Sitio Burle Marx

Heliconia chartacea var. *meeana*

(family Heliconiaceae)

Pencil and gouache on paper, undated (66 x 48.3 cm.)
Collection: Royal Botanic Gardens, Kew

Since the founding of the Heliconia Society International in 1985, heliconias have become increasingly popular as landscaping plants throughout the tropics and subtropics. Margaret Mee discovered this fine species along a tributary of the Rio Negro in Amazonas. It was named in her honour as recently as January 1997 by Dr. John Kress of the Smithsonian Institution.

The drawing is a fine example of Mee's ability to present botanical accuracy within a superb compositional arrangement. The delicate wash of foliage, the subtle coloration, and the striking precision of curves and angles perfectly capture the essence of the plant.

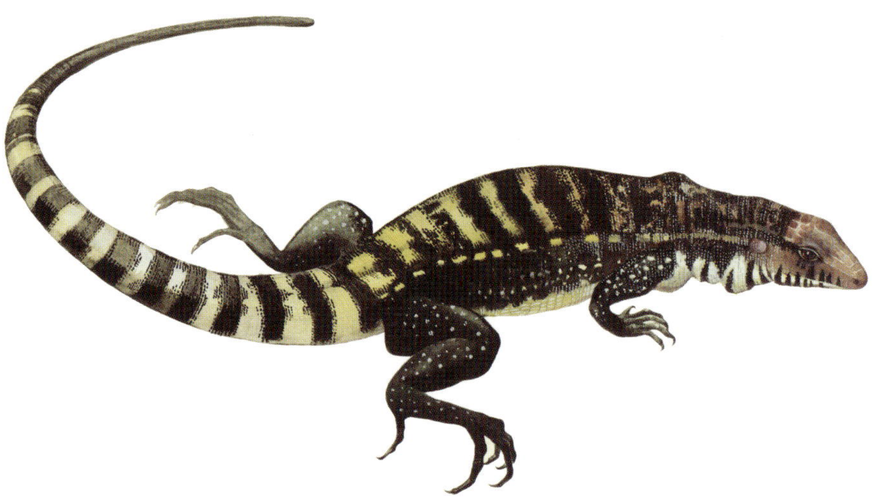

Lizard, field study (Collection: Greville Mee)

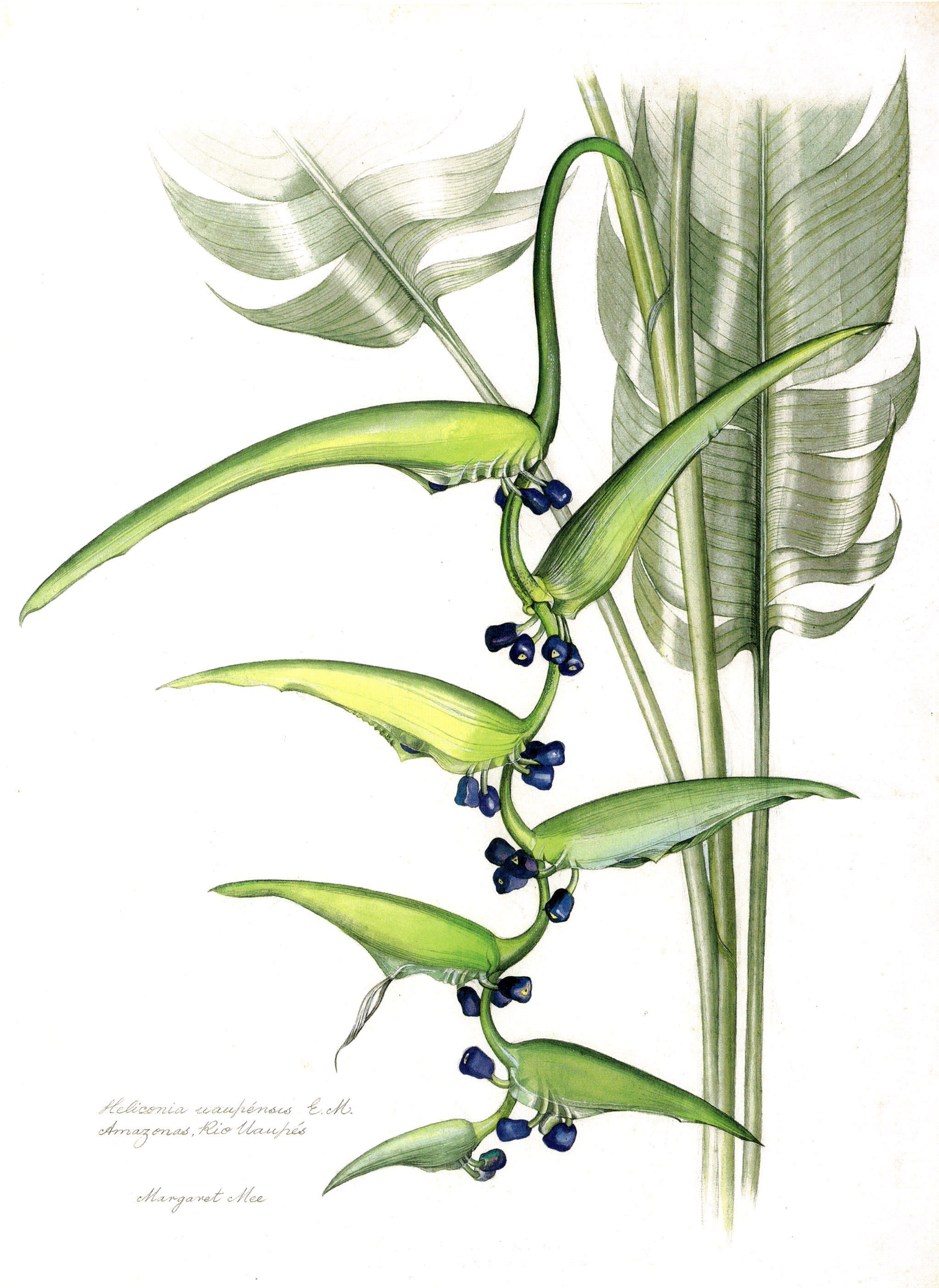
Heliconia uaupénsis E.M.
Amazonas, Rio Uaupés
Margaret Mee

Aechmea huebneri

(family Bromeliaceae)

Pencil and gouache on paper, 1977 (65.7 x 47.9 cm.)
Collection: Royal Botanic Gardens, Kew

Aechmea huebneri grows terrestrially on open ground and epiphytically in the *igapó*. It has an interesting geographical distribution in that it jumps from Amazonia to the eastern coast of Brazil. With its formidable thorns, it is a difficult plant to collect.

Today we collected some fine plants, including an Aechmea *with a long, red inflorescence just turning to fruit, and completely new to me, growing in a tree in the* igapó *bordering the lake.*

M. Mee, *Flowers of the Amazon*

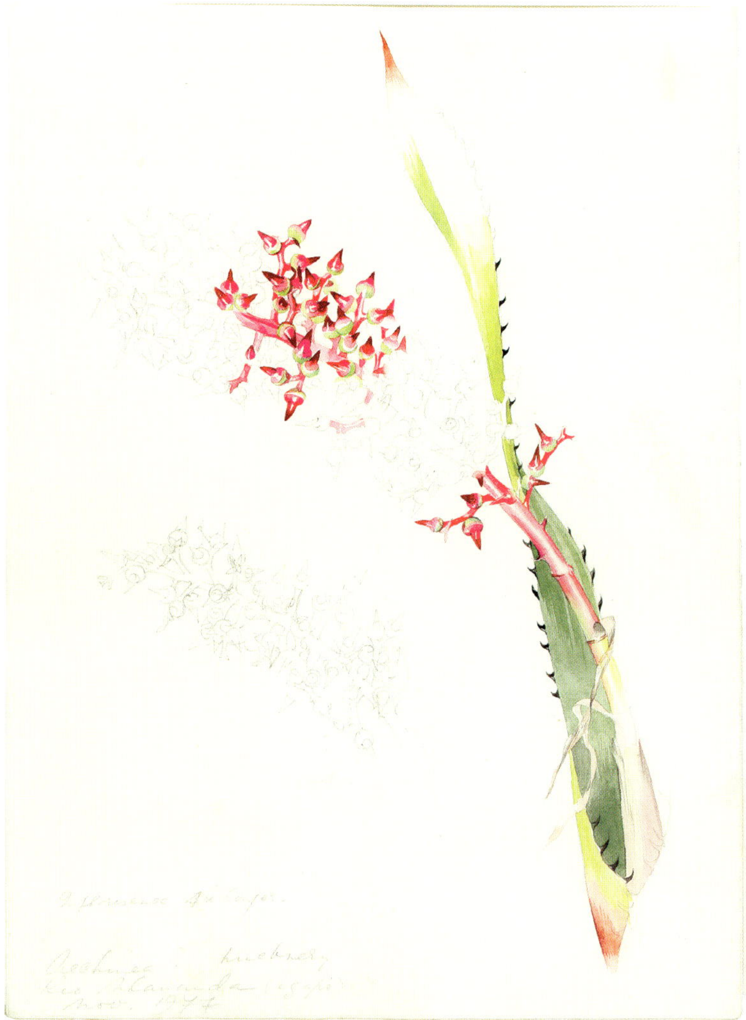

Aechmea huebneri, field sketch

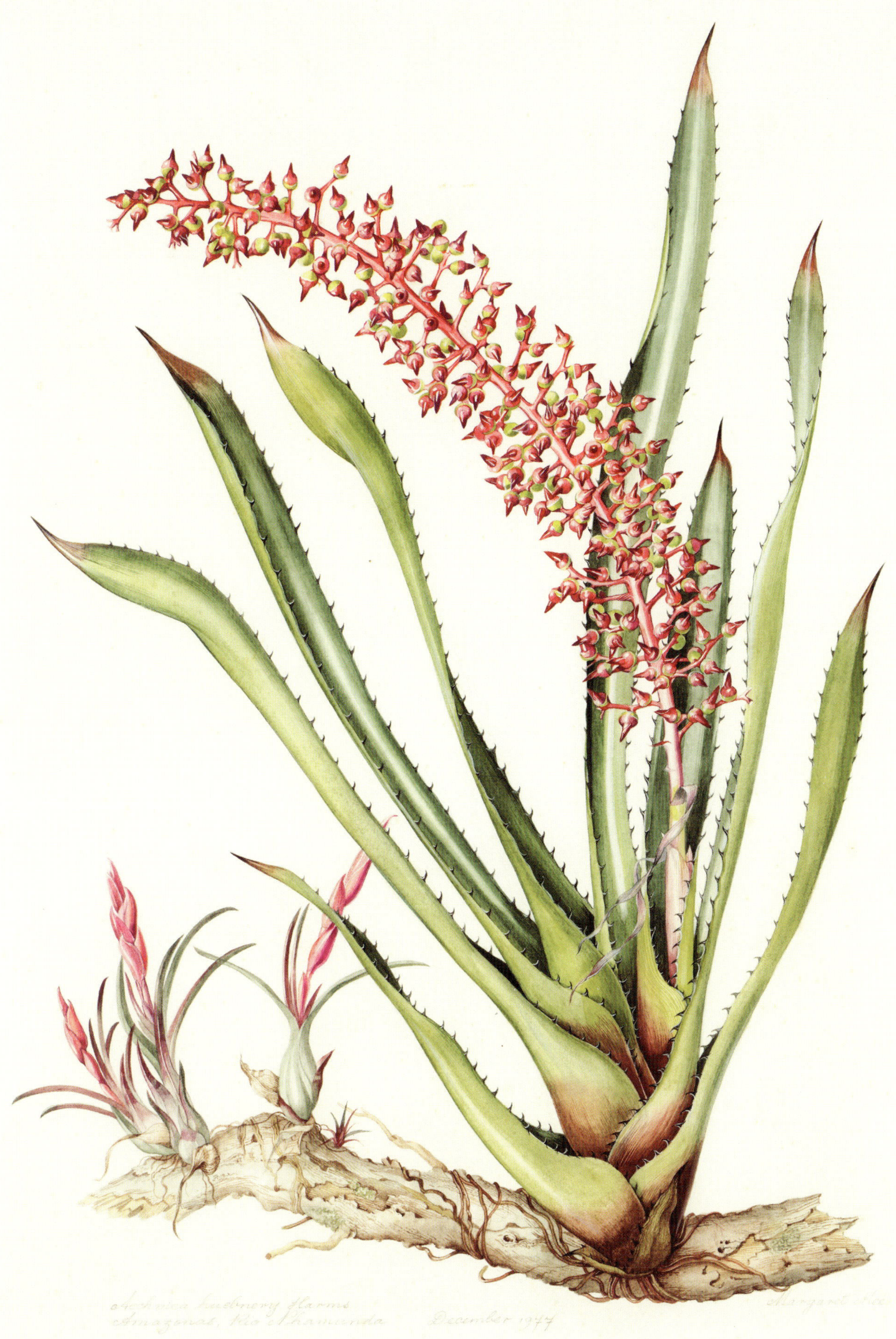
Aechmea huebneri Harms
Amazonas, Rio Nhamunda
December 1977
Margaret Mee

Heterostemon mimosoides

(family Leguminosae)

Pencil and gouache on paper, 1978 (66 x 48.3 cm.)
Collection: Royal Botanic Gardens, Kew

Heterostemon, a small genus of fewer than ten species, is restricted to north-west Brazil and the bordering areas of Colombia and Venezuela. With its abundant orchid-like flowers and splendid foliage, *H. mimosoides* is one of the loveliest of all American leguminous plants.

My encounter with this beautiful tree, with its amethyst flowers and deep green leaves that resemble those of the Mimosa, *was on the Rio Cuieiras, a tributary of the great Rio Negro.* Heterostemon mimosoides *is the tree of which Richard Spruce wrote more than a century ago '... a leguminous tree which was in flower all the way up the river and formed a great ornament to its banks'.*

M. Mee, *Flowers of the Amazon*

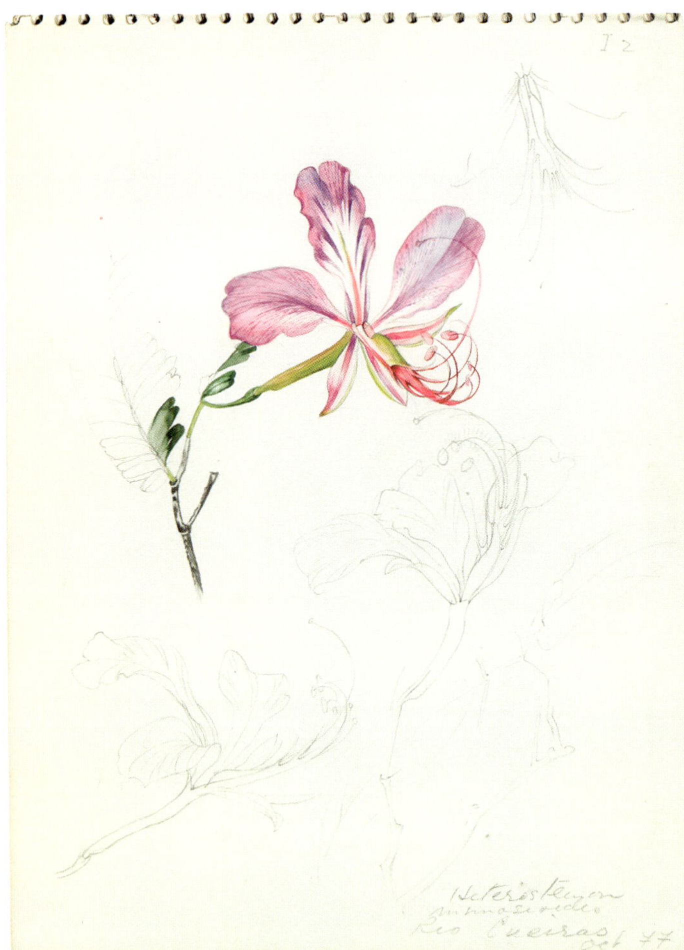

Heterostemon mimosoides, field sketch

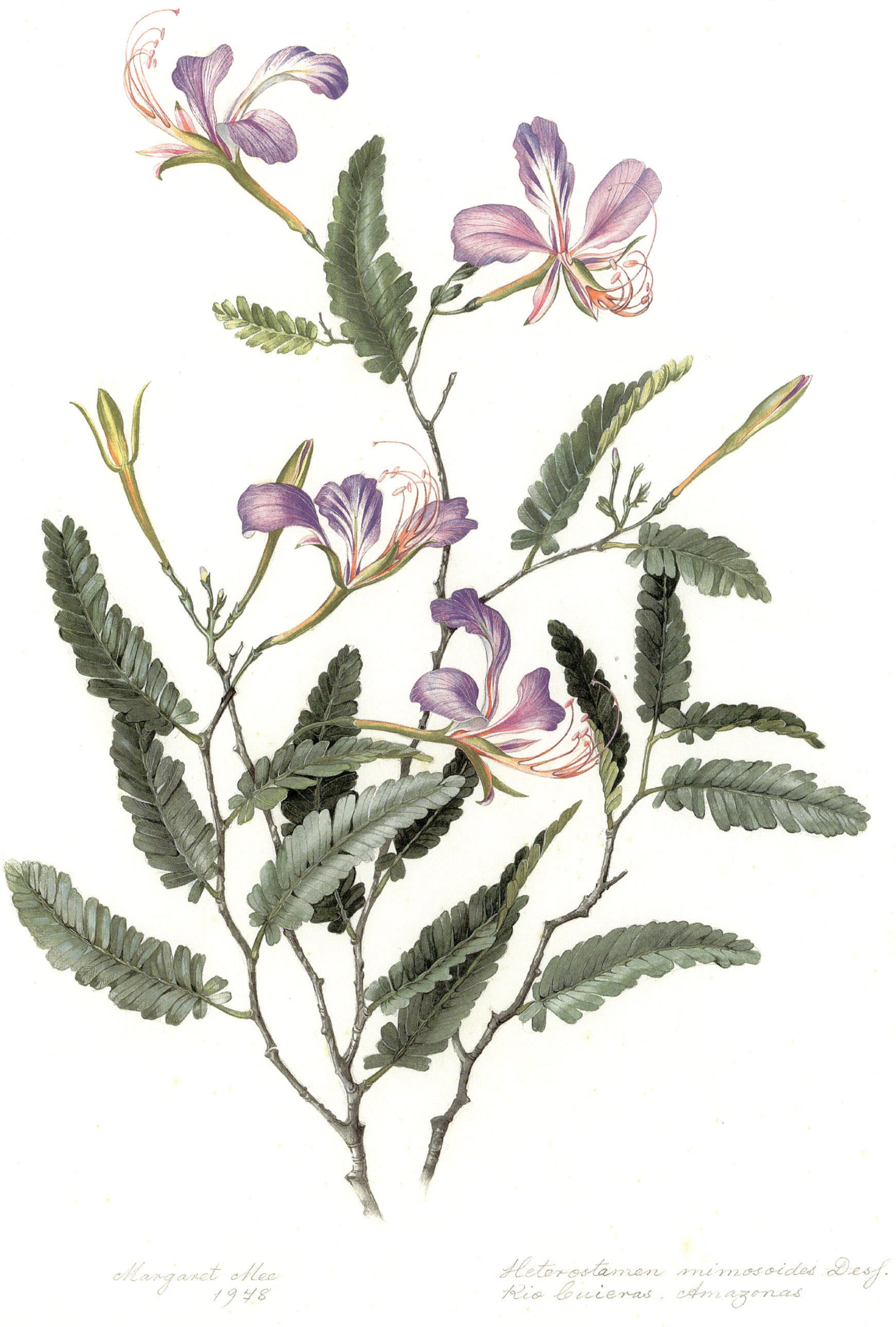
Margaret Mee
1978
Heterostamen mimosoides Desf.
Rio Cuieras, Amazonas

Ionopsis utricularioides

(family Orchidaceae)

Pencil and gouache on paper, 1984 (66 x 47.9 cm.)
Collection: Royal Botanic Gardens, Kew

This very elegant species has been known to botanists since the eighteenth century. Its name is derived from the Greek *ion* (violet) and *opsis* (appearance), referring to the plant's delicate flowers, which resemble violets. These flowers are variable in colour from white to lilac to rose-red, with a striking magenta blotch on the lip.

We paddled among trees and bushes recently devastated by fire, though their wounds had begun to heal, and I found plants which had escaped the conflagration. There were orchids in plenty, the prize of them being Ionopsis utricularioides, *with a mass of fragile violet flowers.*

M. Mee in T. Morrison (ed.), *Margaret Mee: In Search of Flowers of the Amazon Forests*

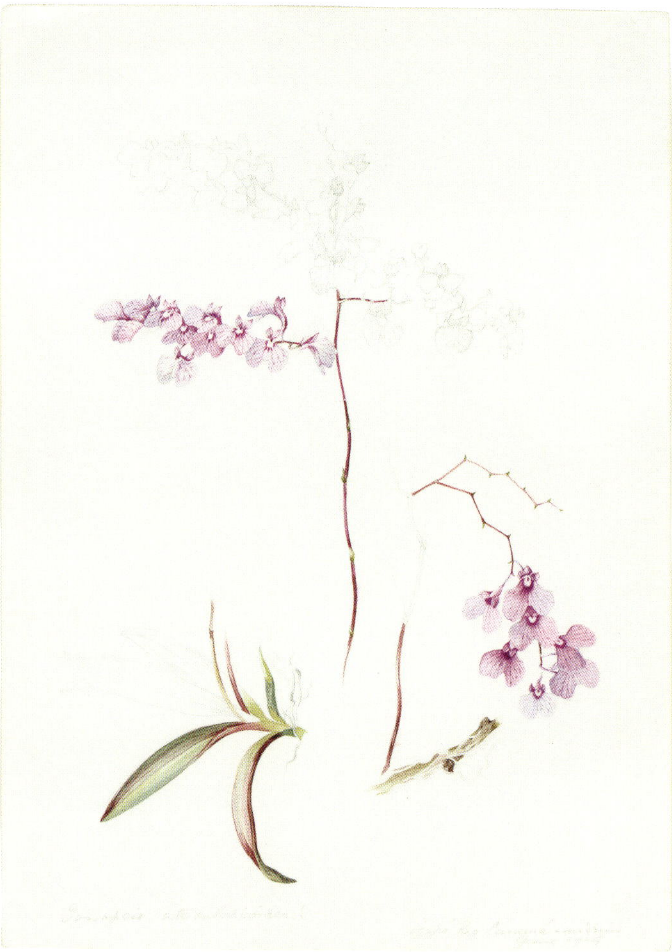

Ionopsis utricularioides, field sketch (Collection: Greville Mee)

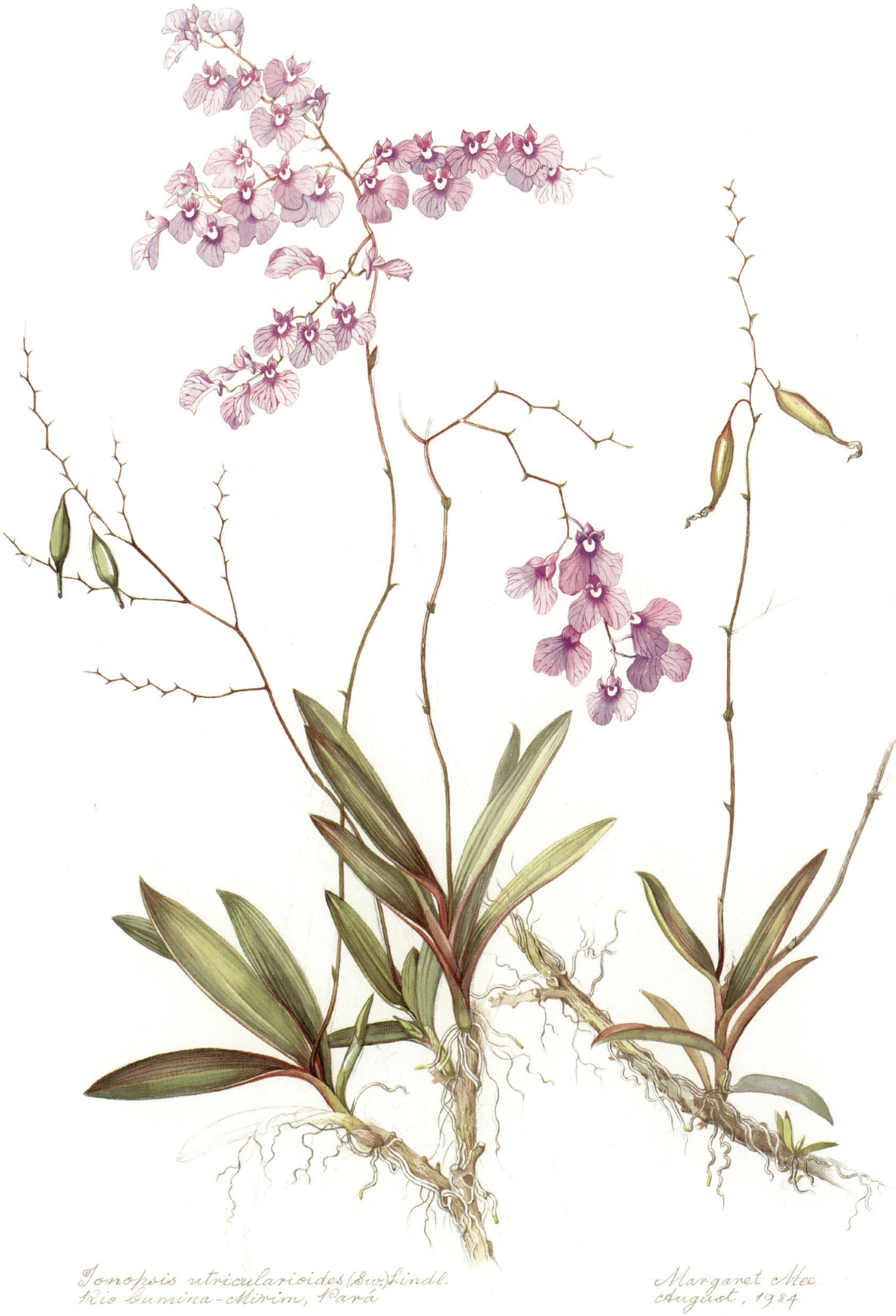
Ionopsis utricularioides (Sw.) Lindl.
Rio Cumina-Mirim, Pará
Margaret Mee
August, 1984

Urospatha sagittifolia

(family Araceae)

Pencil and gouache on paper, 1976 (75.9 x 47.9 cm.)
Collection: Royal Botanic Gardens, Kew

This striking wetland plant features elongated, corkscrew-tipped inflorescences and large triangular leaves. Several species of a related genus, *Cyrtosperma* from south-east Asia, also produce curiously twisted floral spathes, suggesting ancient links between the plants of the Old and New Worlds.

Many years ago I voyaged on the beautiful Rio Uaupés where Richard Spruce had explored more than a hundred years ago. Nature was exuberant. In the swamps beside the path, a strange aroid thrust long stems with arrow shaped leaves. I was able to trace the subtle lines and follow the dark colours.

M. Mee, *Flowers of the Amazon*

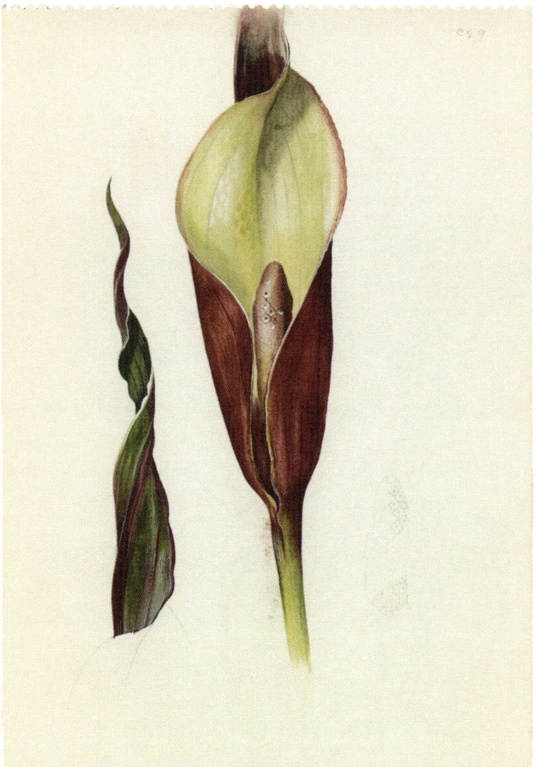

Urospatha sagittifolia, field sketch

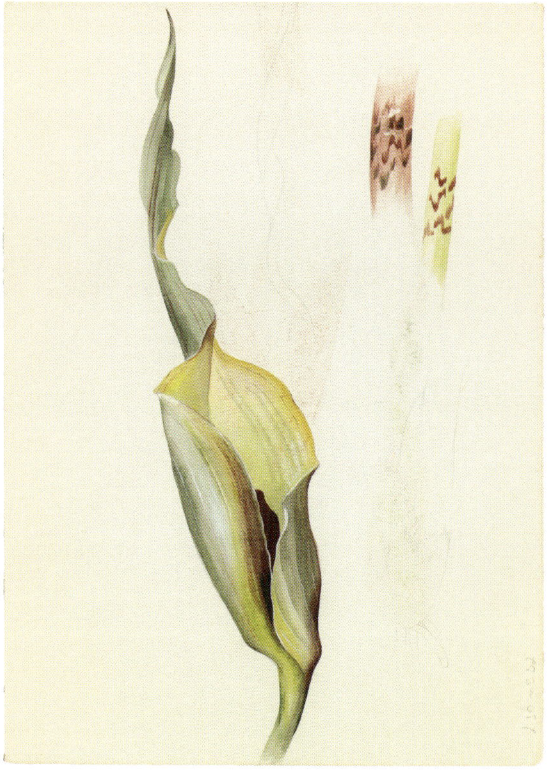

Urospatha sagittifolia, field sketch

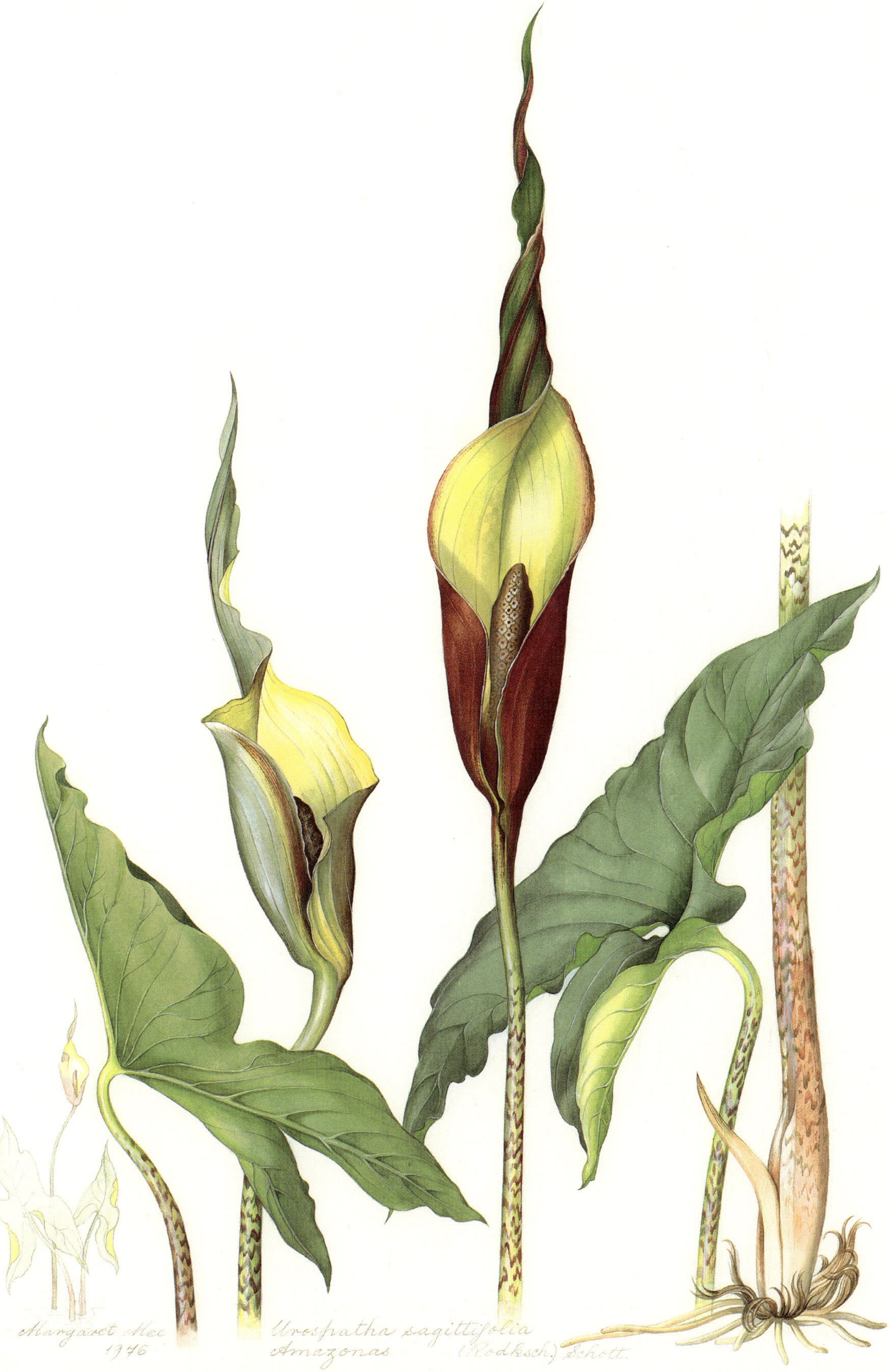
Margaret Mee
1976
Urospatha sagittifolia
Amazonas
(Rodksch.) Schott.

Scuticaria steelii

(family Orchidaceae)

Pencil and gouache on paper, 1972 (66 x 48.3 cm.)
Collection: Royal Botanic Gardens, Kew

Scuticaria, a genus of only five species, derives its name from the Latin *scutica* (whip), which refers to the plant's long, whip-like leaves. *Scuticaria steelii* was named after Matthew Steele, who discovered this unusual orchid in Guyana in 1836. Mee's specimen was collected along the Rio Negro, where it was found growing on a *Jará* palm.

It has been a fantastic trip and my finds have been very good – many beautiful orchids including the lovely perfumed Scuticaria steelii, *yellow, spotted with chestnut, whose cylindrical leaves hang a metre long.*

M. Mee, *Flowers of the Amazon*

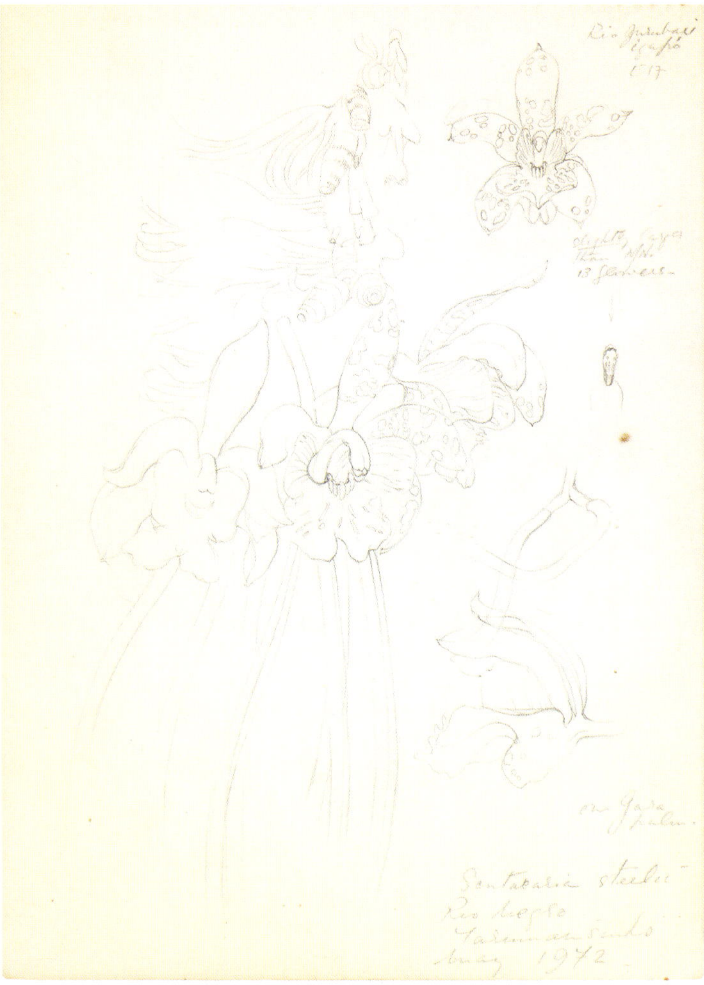

Scuticaria steelii, field sketch

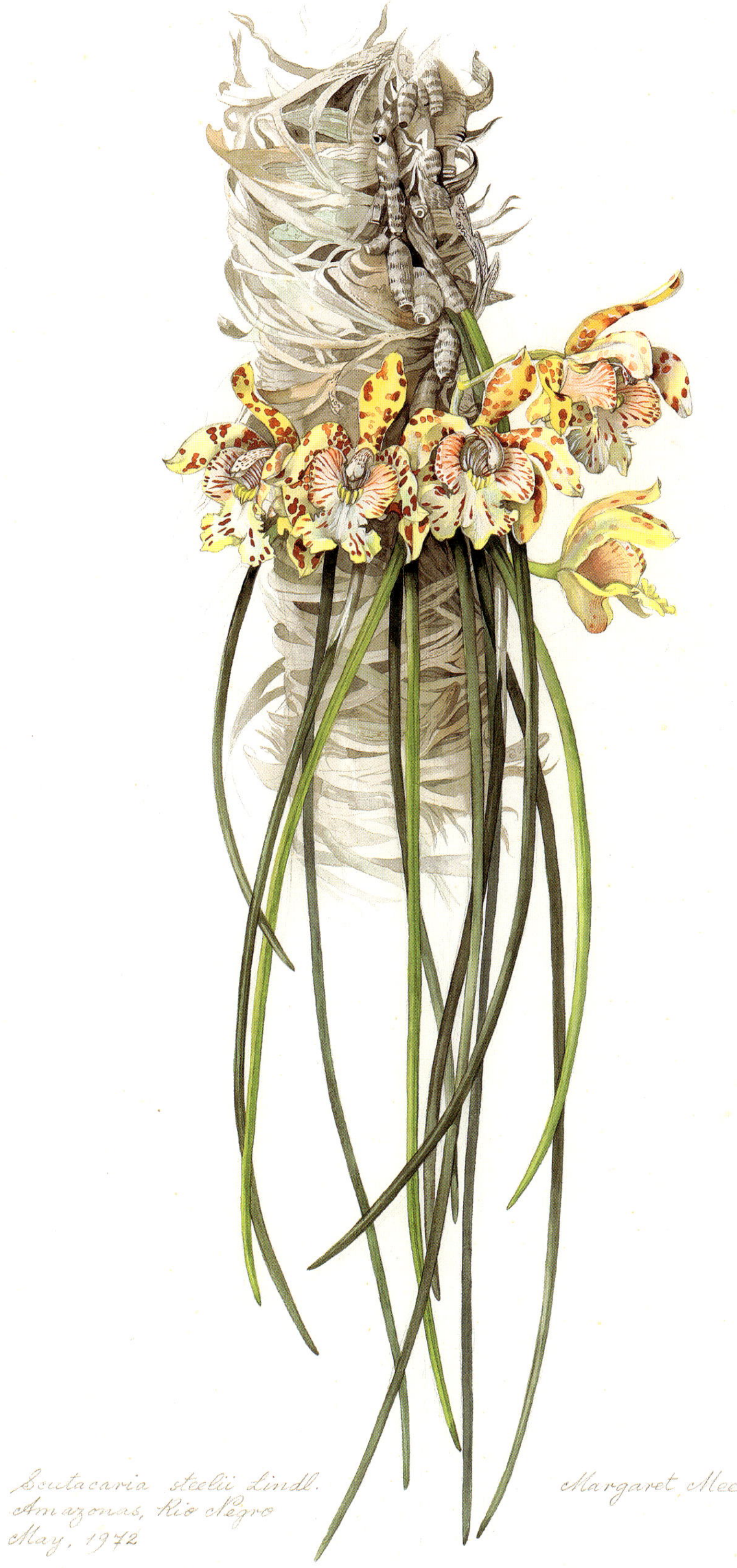

Scutacaria steelii Lindl.
Amazonas, Rio Negro
May, 1972
Margaret Mee

Clusia grandiflora

(family Clusiaceae)

Pencil and gouache on paper, 1987 (66 x 48.3 cm.)
Collection: Royal Botanic Gardens, Kew

The Clusiaceae family includes trees, shrubs, and lianas known for their viscous sap. The largest genus, *Clusia,* is found only in tropical America. The habitat of *Clusia grandiflora* has a somewhat restricted range. It includes eastern Amazonia and has been found in Surinam, Guyana, and the Brazilian state of Pará in the region of Belém.

In the early hours of the morning the river's face was covered with a dense white mist ...the sky began to get a first flush of rose and gold, the mists lifted like a gossamer curtain, and the chill humidity gave way to the burning heat of day. We were passing the most wonderful, flowered-filled forests. There was an abundance of clusias with white blossoms.

M. Mee, *Flowers of the Amazon*

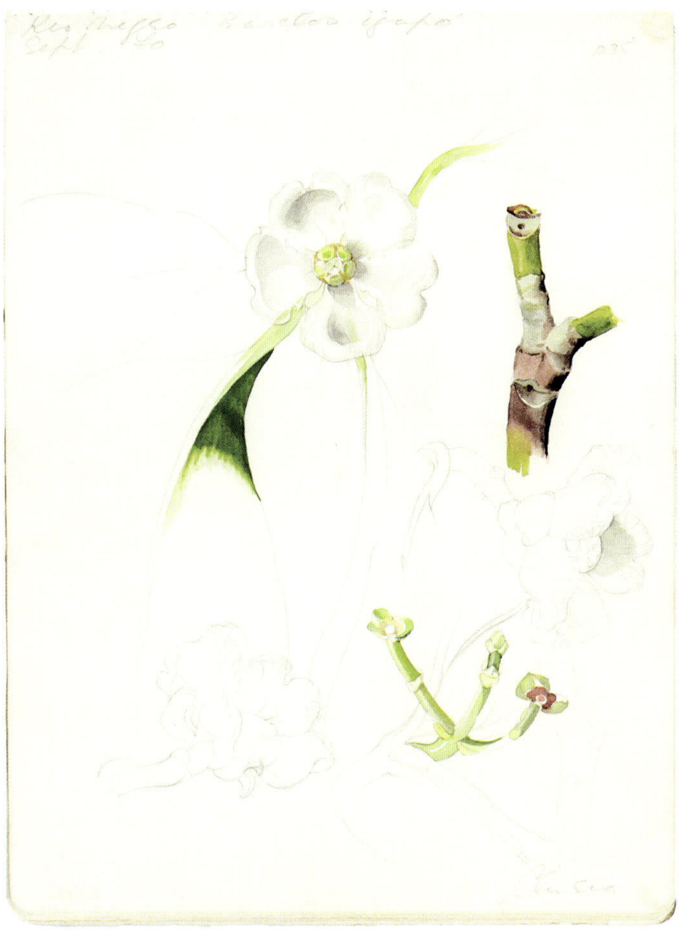

Clusia grandiflora, field sketch

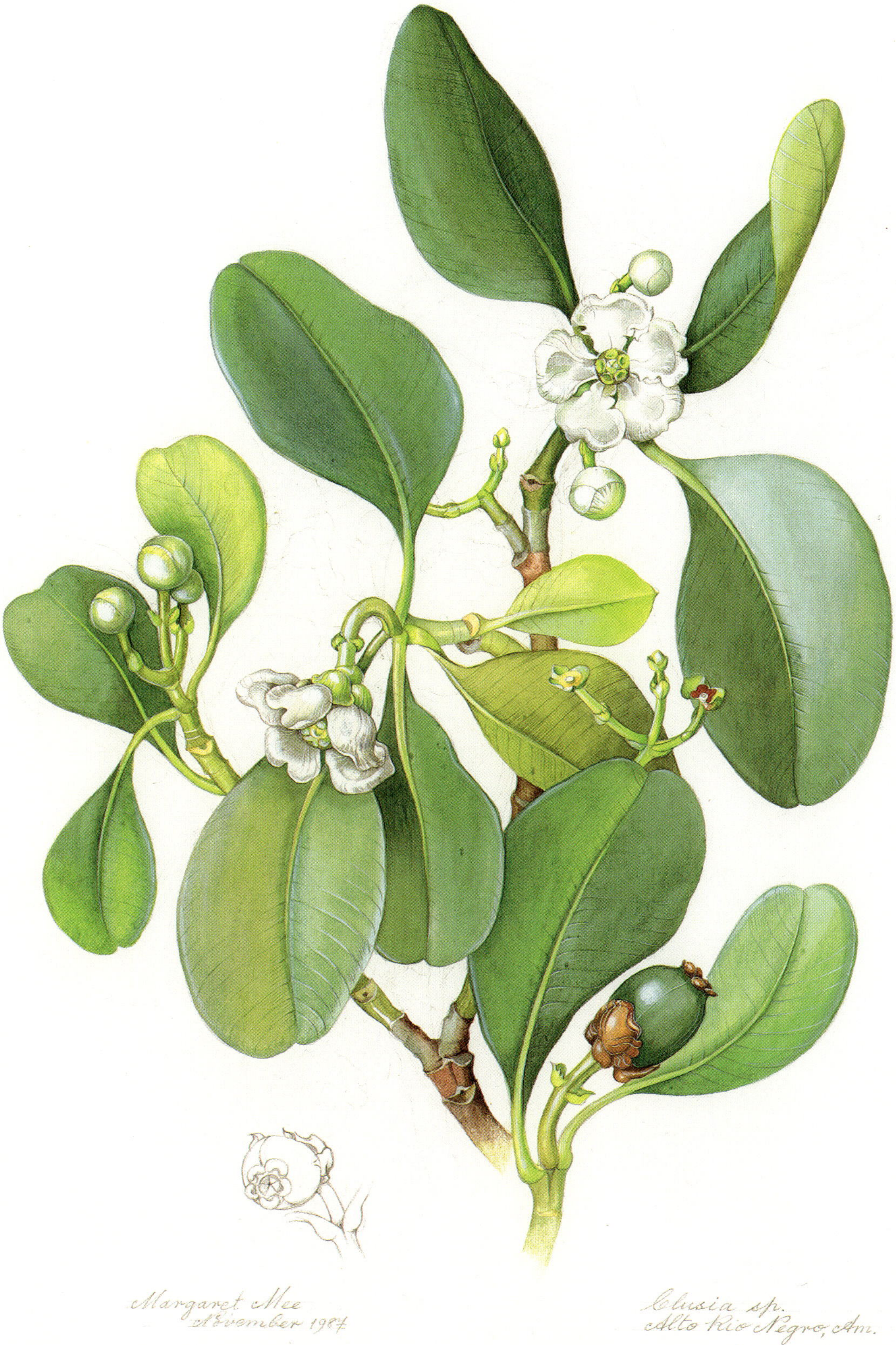
Margaret Mee
November 1987
Clusia sp.
Alto Rio Negro, Am.

Catasetum punctatum

(family Orchidaceae)

Pencil and gouache on paper, 1974 (66 x 47.9 cm.)
Collection: Royal Botanic Gardens, Kew

This rare epiphytic orchid was introduced into cultivation by L'Horticulture Internationale, the Belgian nursery that Jean Linden established in the mid 1800s. Linden supported the exploration of South America by financing expeditions in search of new and rare orchids.

... the surface of the water was like a mirror, and reality and reflections were almost indistinguishable one from the other. Orchids and bromeliads grew there in profusion, and amongst them I was fortunate enough to find Catasetum punctatum. *I was able to paint these flowers before the light faded, after which we supped on piranhas.*

M. Mee, *Flowers of the Amazon*

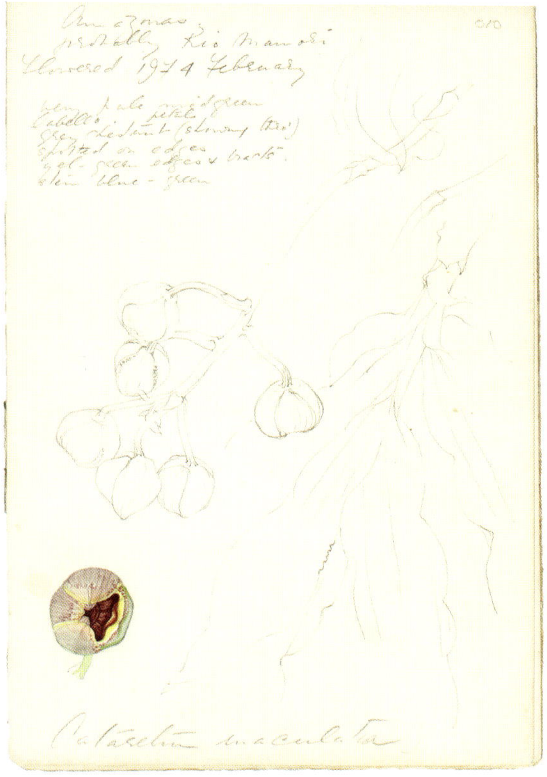

Catasetum punctatum, field sketch

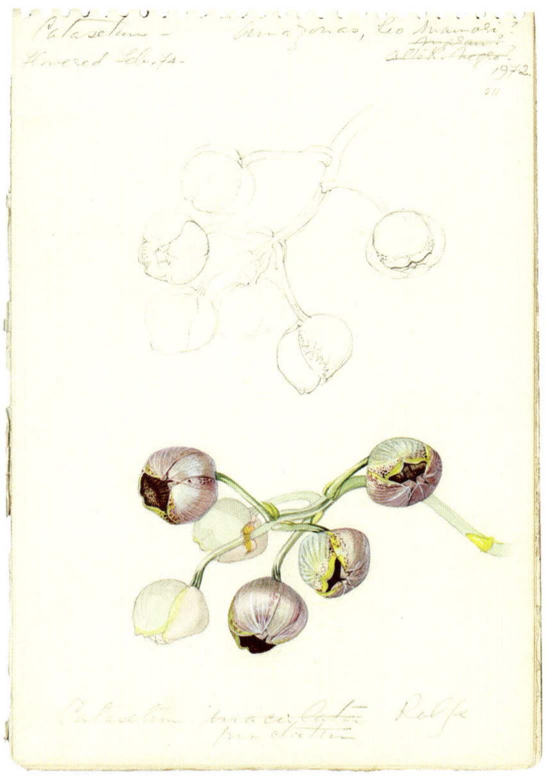

Catasetum punctatum, field sketch

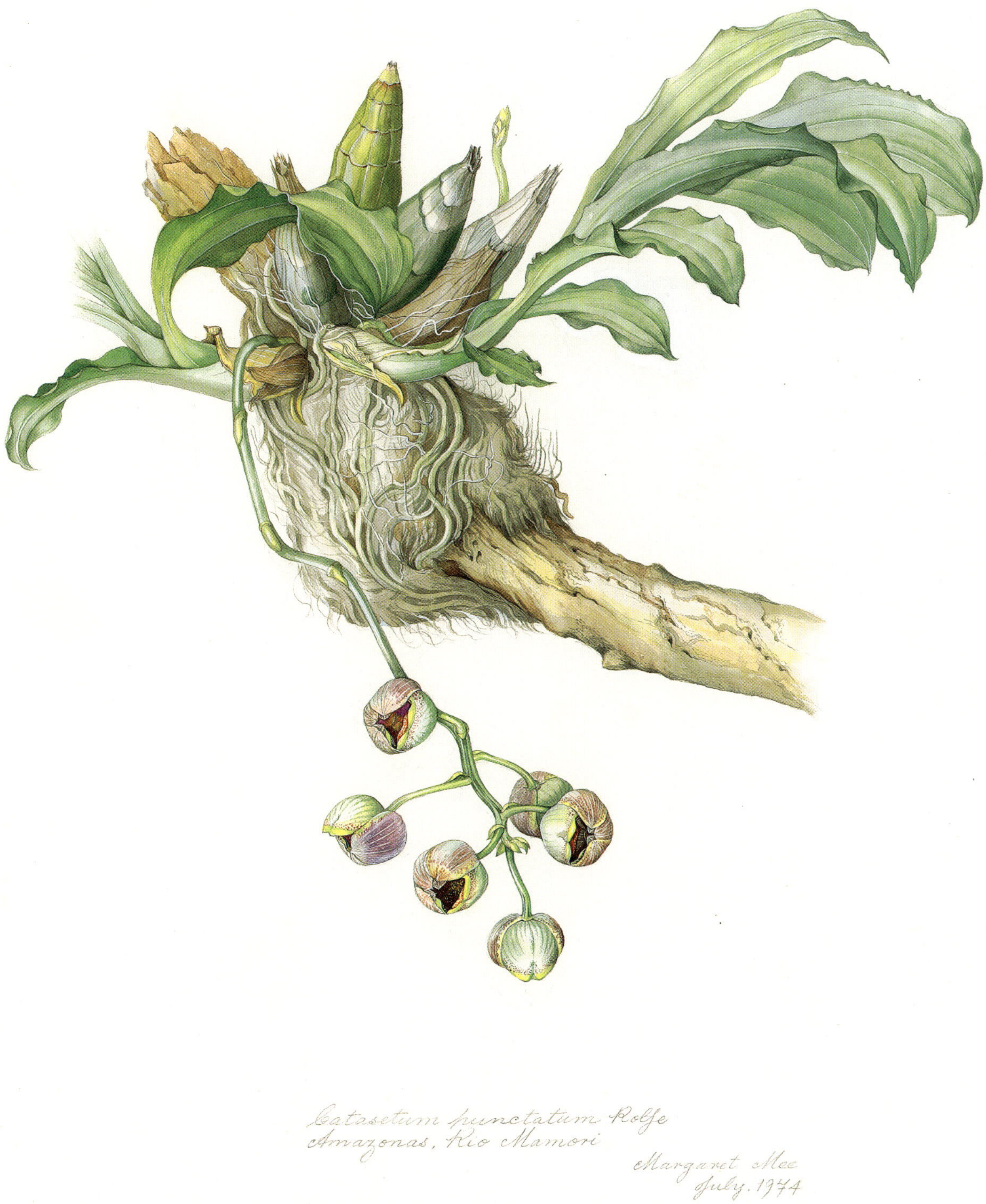
Catasetum punctatum Rolfe
Amazonas, Rio Mamori
Margaret Mee
July. 1974

Catasetum saccatum

(family Orchidaceae)

Pencil and gouache on paper, 1977 (66 x 47.9 cm.)
Collection: Royal Botanic Gardens, Kew

Note the yellow-green female flowers of this orchid and the more numerous maroon-to-brown male ones. With her skillful use of highlights and shadows, Mee allows one to understand the thick texture of the flowers and the gentle curves of the leaves. This highly variable species is distributed throughout Peru, Brazil, and the Guianas.

The masculine flowers of this strangely beautiful plant are completely different from the female flowers, imitating dark bats with outspread wings. The modest female flowers resemble the green hoods of elfins. Both forms grow on the same plant.

M. Mee, *Flowers of the Amazon*

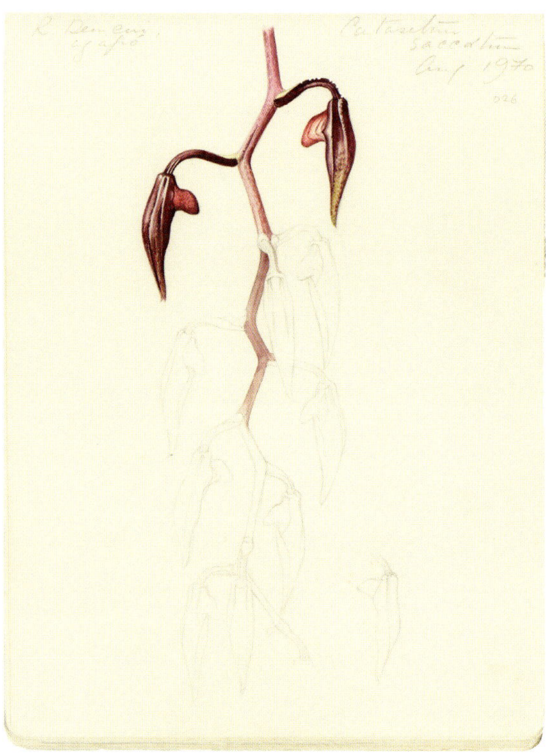

Catasetum saccatum, field sketch

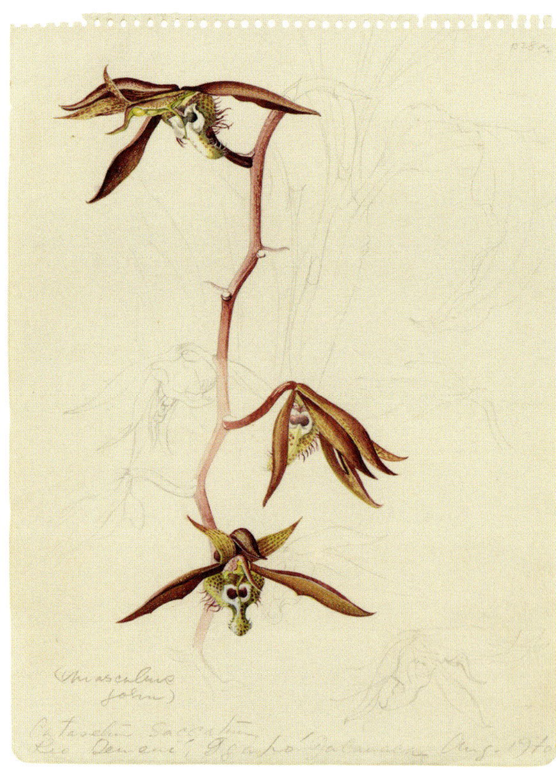

Catasetum saccatum, field sketch

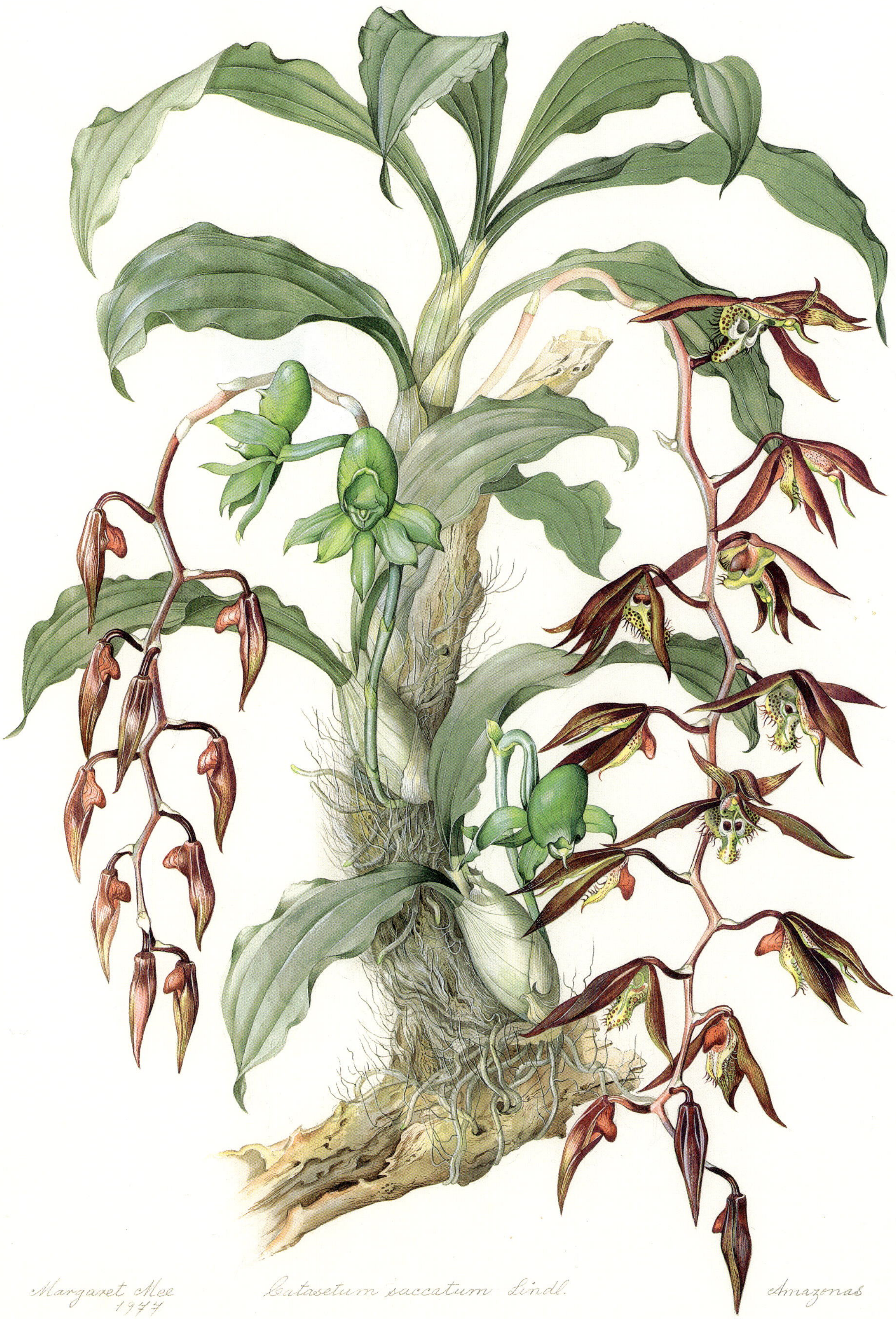
Margaret Mee
1977
Catasetum saccatum Lindl.
Amazonas

Aechmea meeana

(family Bromeliaceae)

Pencil and gouache on paper, 1978 (66 x 48.3 cm.)
Collection: Royal Botanic Gardens, Kew

Lyman B. Smith, the world's leading authority on Bromeliaceae, named *Aechmea meeana* in honour of its discoverer, Margaret Mee. Each leathery leaf of this plant narrows to a point ending in a woody black spine and is notched along its margins with large, deep purple spines. The leaves are covered with water-absorbing scales, a characteristic common to all bromeliads. This rare species is known scientifically only from Mee's collections.

Bento plunged into the river and climbed into the tree fork, my bushknife between his teeth. He carefully picked out the hairy spiders from the leaf-cups, then hacked at the woody roots. To free himself from the tormenting ants he plunged into the river, before returning for another plant of this new species.

M. Mee, *Flowers of the Amazon*

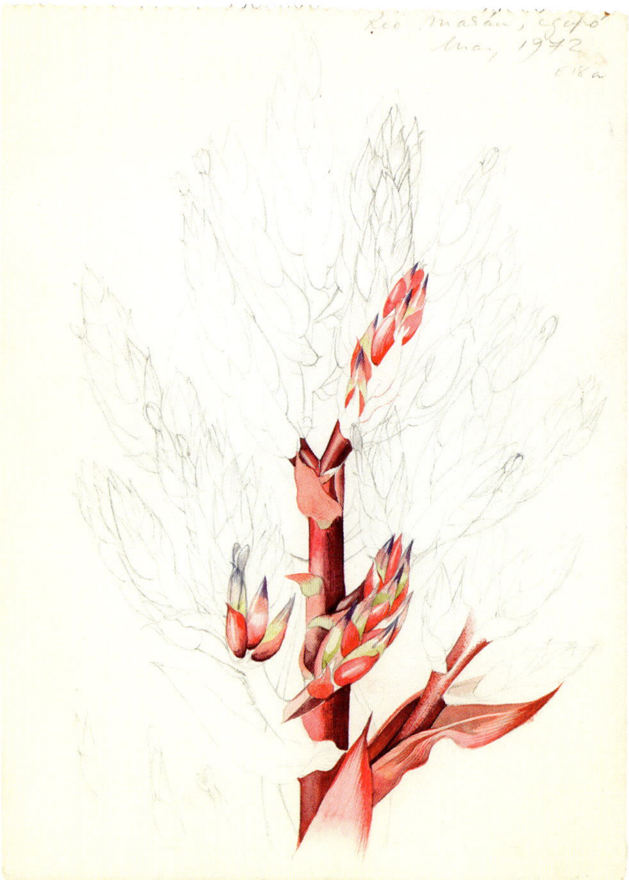

Aechmea meeana, field sketch

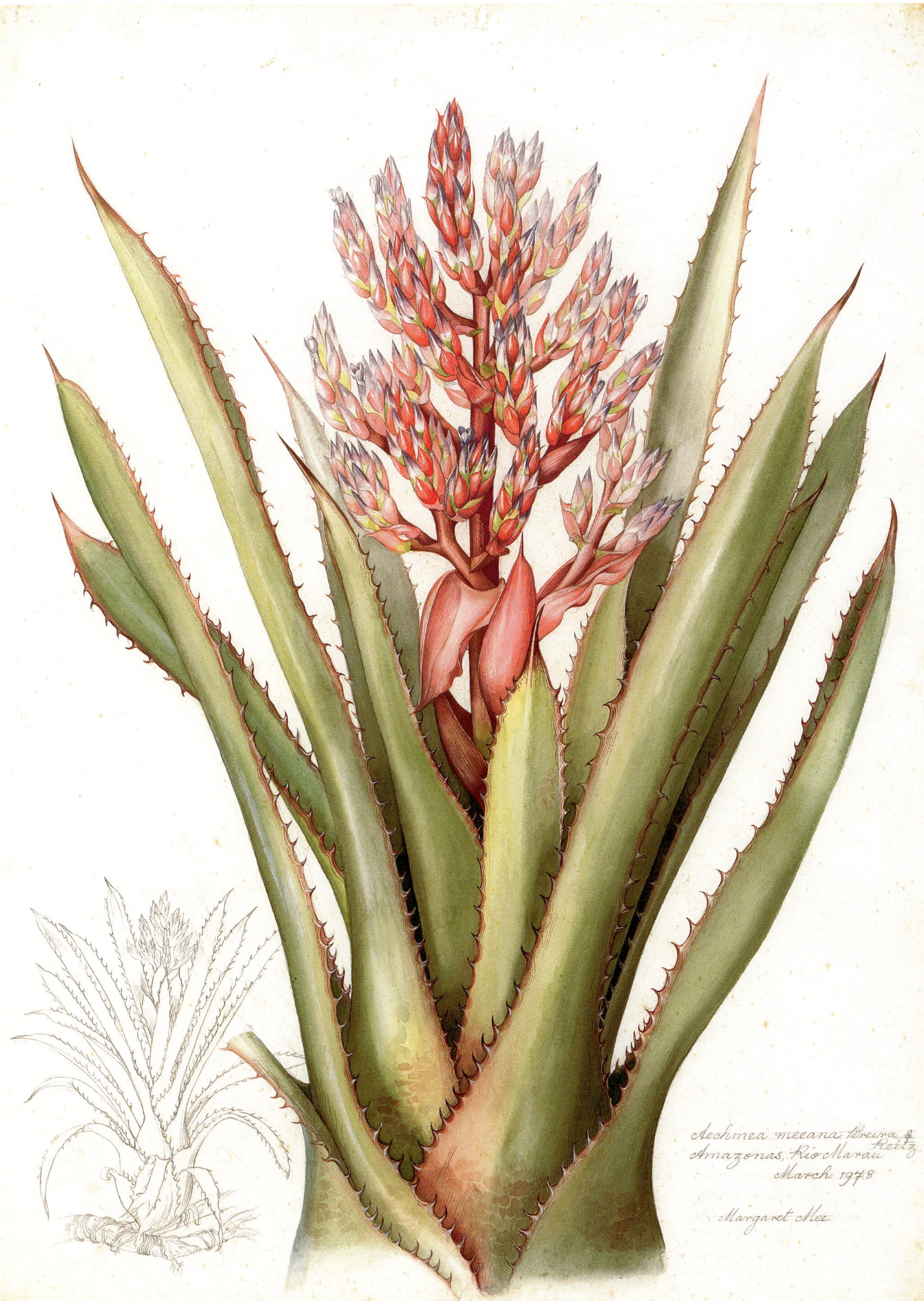
Aechmea meeana Pereira & Reitz
Amazonas, Rio Marau
March 1978
Margaret Mee

Vriesea 'Charlotte'

(family Bromeliaceae)

Carolina de Bassi, 2003 Margaret Mee Scholar
Pencil and gouache on paper, 2003 (74.4 x 52.5 cm.)
Shirley Sherwood Collection

The genus *Vriesea*, named after the nineteenth-century Dutch botanist, W. H. de Vriese, was established by the British taxonomist John Lindley in 1843, and contains more than 225 species, with new ones constantly being discovered. These plants are distributed over a large area from Mexico, Central America and the West Indies to Peru, Bolivia, Argentina and Brazil.

Seeking dappled light combined with good air circulation, vrieseas grow epiphytically on tree branches in the rainforest. Their broad leaves form vase-shaped rosettes, and the highly coloured floral bracts remain vivid for weeks. 'Charlotte' is a cultivated hybrid from unknown parents.

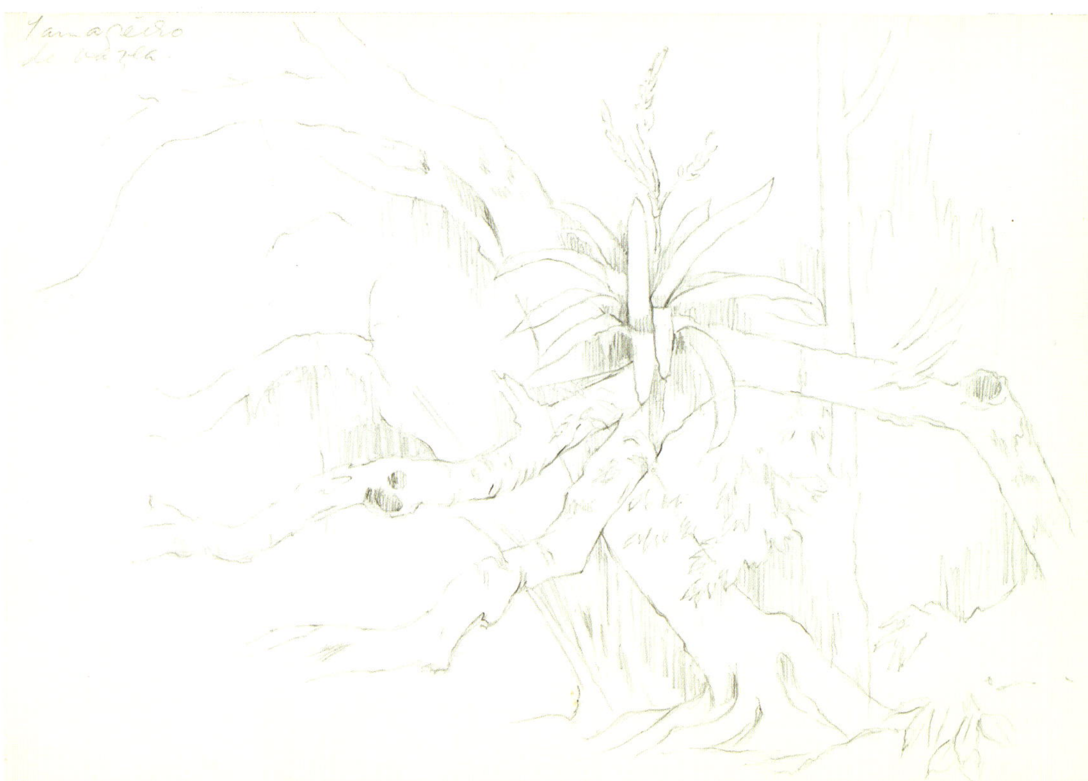

Bromeliads blooming in the *várzea* (annually flooded forest), field sketch

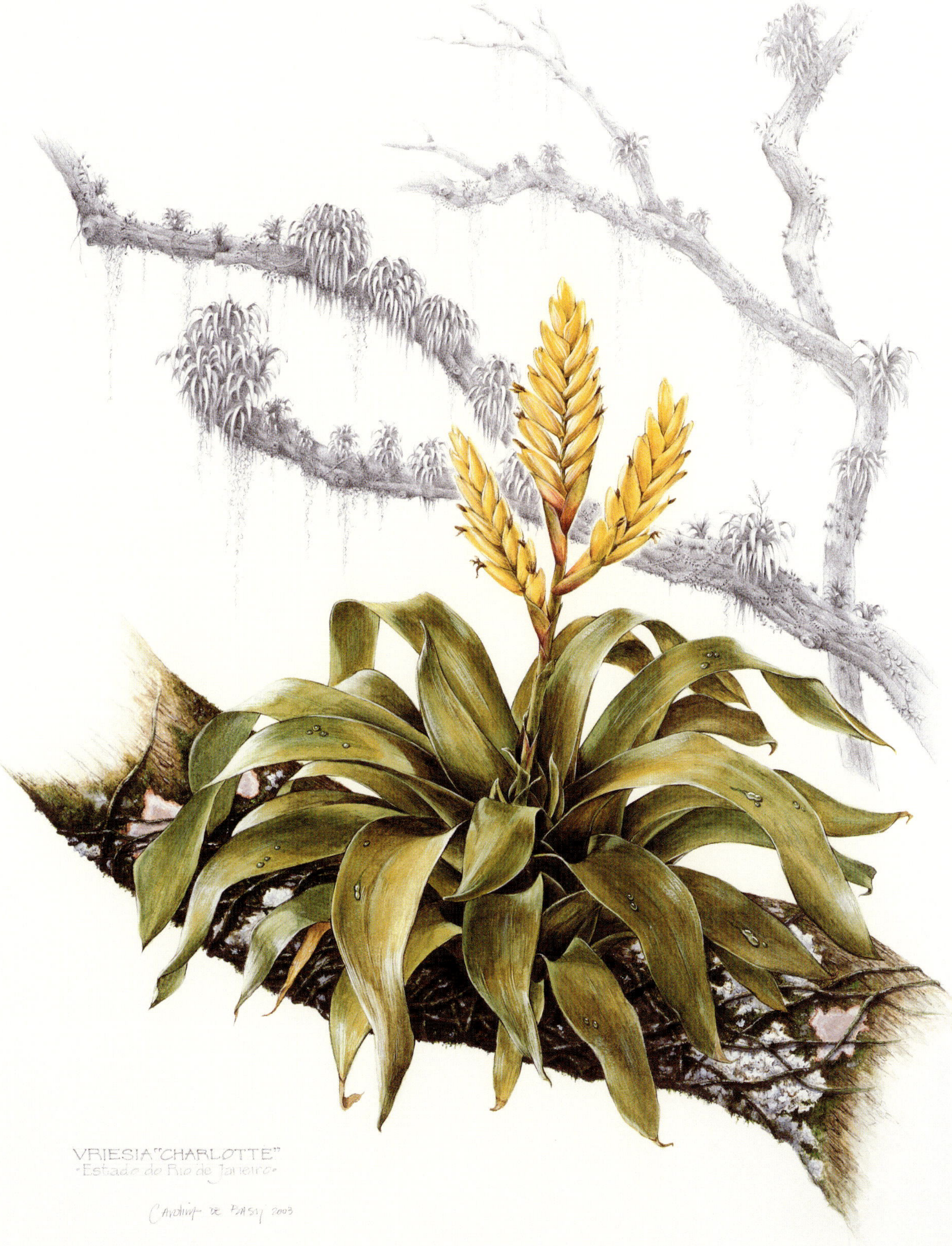

VRIESIA "CHARLOTTE"
•Estado do Rio de Janeiro•

Richard Spruce

In 1849, the British explorer and plant collector Richard Spruce began fifteen continuous years of arduous exploration along the entire length of the Amazon. Arguably the greatest of all Amazon explorers and Margaret Mee's primary inspiration, Spruce made the world aware of South American flora through a collection of Amazonian plants that remains unequalled. Margaret Mee's itineraries often followed his and quotes from Spruce's *Notes of a Botanist on the Amazon and Andes*, a classic of travel literature, are sprinkled throughout Mee's diaries.

In 1848, just one year prior to Spruce's epic journeys, the Royal Botanic Gardens, Kew opened its Museum of Economic Botany. It was truly a "cabinet of curiosities", with plants and their products, artifacts, and drawings displayed in a somewhat chaotic fashion. *"I shall send you whatever I can obtain here for your museum,"* wrote Spruce in a letter of 1851 to Sir William Hooker, Kew's Director. Crate after crate was shipped to London, revealing a fascinating array of clothing, weapons, ornaments, utilitarian artifacts, and ceremonial objects accompanied by copious notes on their manufacture and use.

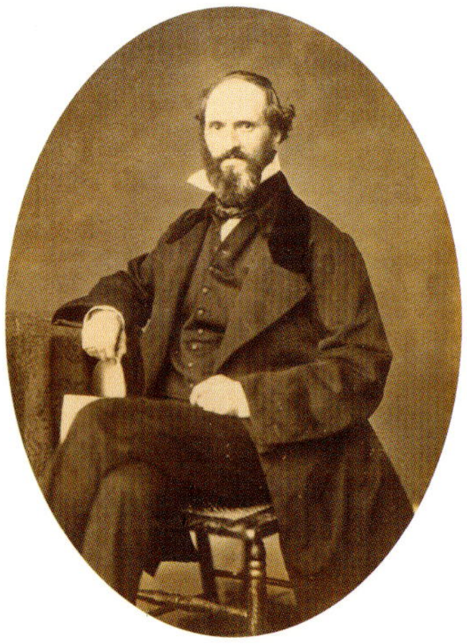

Richard Spruce, 1817 – 1893

Quiver

Collected by R. Spruce, c. 1850
Centre for Economic Botany; RBG, Kew

Case containing poisoned arrows for use with blow guns. Made by the Catauixi Indians, Amazonas.

Shield

Collected by R. Spruce, c. 1852
Centre for Economic Botany; RBG, Kew

Used by the Uaupé Indians to deflect arrows. Made of *sipo* or vine called "Timbo-titica" and partially smeared with pitch from the plant *Symphonia globulifera*. Collected from the Rio Uaupés, a tributary of the Rio Negro.

Gourds of curare

Collected by R. Spruce, c. 1852
Centre for Economic Botany; RBG, Kew

Containing poison from the bark of *Strychnos*. For use with darts and arrows associated with blow guns.

Calabash

Collected by R. Spruce, c. 1850
Centre for Economic Botany; RBG, Kew

Small bucket used on board canoes for holding water. Made from a hollowed calabash with a handle of woven piassaba fiber attached to two crossed bands of netted *curana* cloth.

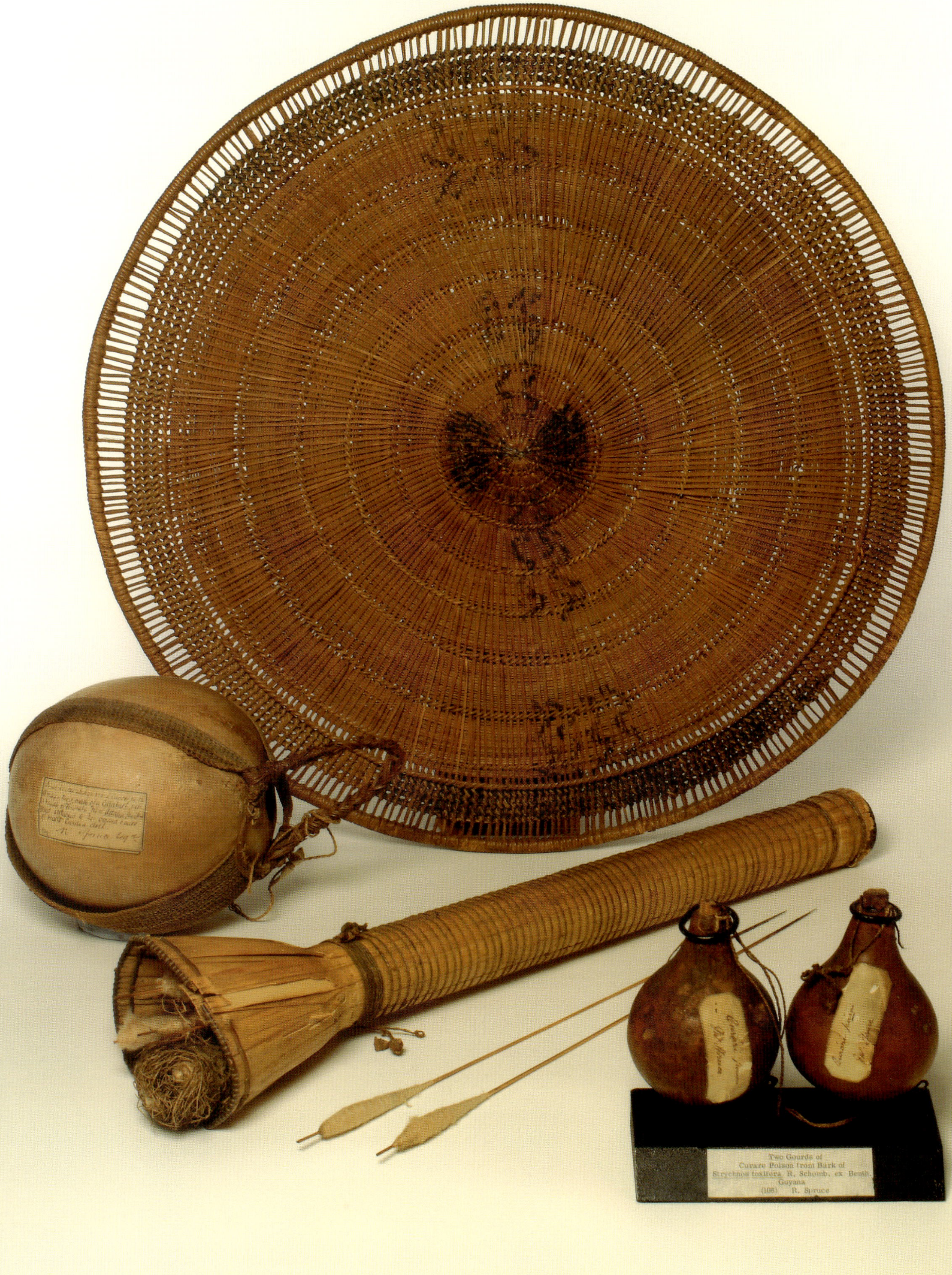
Two Gourds of
Curare Poison from Bark of
Strychnos toxifera R. Schomb. ex Benth.
Guyana
(108) R. Spruce

Selected Bibliography

Blunt, Wilfrid, and William T. Stearn. *The Art of Botanical Illustration.* Rev. and enl. Woodbridge, England: Antique Collectors' Club in association with the Royal Botanic Gardens, Kew, 1994.

Desmond, Ray. *Kew: The History of the Royal Botanic Gardens.* London: Harvill Press and Royal Botanic Gardens, Kew, 1995.

Elliott, Brent. *Treasures of the Royal Horticultural Society.* London: Herbert Press in association with the Royal Horticultural Society, 1994.

Evans, Anne-Marie, and Donn Evans. *An Approach to Botanical Painting in Watercolour.* Rutland: Hannaford and Evans, 1993.

Goulding, Michael. *Amazon: The Flooded Forest.* New York: Sterling Publishing Co., 1990.

Hemming, John. *Amazon Frontier: The Defeat of the Brazilian Indians.* Cambridge: Harvard University Press, 1987.

Hemming, John. *Die If You Must: Brazilian Indians in the Twentieth Century.* London: Macmillan, 2003.

Lack, H. Walter. *Ein Garten Eden: Meisterwerke der botanischen Illustration* (Garden Eden: Masterpieces of Botanical Illustration). English translation by Martin Walters. Köln, N.Y.: Taschen, 2001.

Mee, Margaret. *Flowers of the Amazon.* Rio de Janeiro: Distribuidora Record, 1980.

Mee, Margaret. *Flowers of the Brazilian Forests.* London: The Tryon Gallery, 1968.

Morrison, Tony (ed.). *Margaret Mee: In Search of Flowers of the Amazon Forests.* Woodbridge: Nonesuch Expeditions, 1988.

Rix, Martyn. *The Art of the Plant World: The Great Botanical Illustrators and Their Work.* Woodstock, N.Y.: Overlook Press, 1981.

Saunders, Gil. *Picturing Plants: An Analytical History of Botanical Illustration.* Berkeley: University of California Press in association with the Victoria and Albert Museum, London, 1995.

Schultes, R.E. "Margaret Mee and Richard Spruce." *Naturalist* 115: 146-148 (1990).

Sherwood, Shirley. *Contemporary Botanical Artists.* London: Weidenfeld and Nicolson in Association with the Royal Botanic Gardens, Kew, 1996.

Sherwood, Shirley. *A Passion for Plants, Contemporary Botanical Masterworks from the Shirley Sherwood Collection.* London: Cassell & Co., 2001.

Sitwell, Sacheverell, and Wilfrid Blunt. *Great Flower Books 1700-1900, A Bibliographical Record of Two Centuries of Finely Illustrated Flower Books.* New York: Atlantic Monthly Press, 1990.

Spruce, Richard. *Notes of a Botanist on the Amazon and Andes.* (ed. Alfred Russel Wallace). London: Macmillan and Co. Ltd, 1908.

Stearn, William T. *Flower Artists of Kew,* London: Herbert Press in association with the Royal Botanic Gardens, Kew, 1990.

Stiff, Ruth L. A. *Flowers from the Royal Gardens of Kew.* Hanover: University Press of New England, 1988.

Stiff, Ruth L. A. *Margaret Mee: Return to the Amazon.* London: The Stationery Office, 1996.

Tomasi, Luci Tongiorgi. *An Oak Spring Flora: Flower Illustration from the Fifteenth Century to the Present Time, A Selection of the Rare Books, Manuscripts and Works of Art in the Collection of Rachel Lambert Mellon.* Upperville, Va.: Oak Spring Garden Library, 1997.

First published in 2004 by
Royal Botanic Gardens, Kew
Richmond, Surrey, TW9 3AB, UK
www.kew.org

SOFT BOUND ISBN 1 84246 077 3
HARD BOUND ISBN 1 84246 078 1

Designed by Jeff Eden for
Media Resources, Information Services Department,
Royal Botanic Gardens, Kew

Printed by B·A·S Printers Limited
Salisbury, Wiltshire, United Kingdom

Digital images kindly provided by
Oppenheimer Editions, LLC, Chicago
and
Royal Botanic Gardens, Kew

COVER IMAGE
Gustavia augusta

For information or to purchase all Kew titles please visit
www.kewbooks.com or email publishing@kew.org